Math
DictioNary
for kids

Math DictioNary
for kids

THE ESSENTIAL GUIDE TO MATH TERMS, STRATEGIES, AND TABLES

THERESA R. FITZGERALD

PRUFROCK PRESS INC.
WACO, TEXAS

Library of Congress Cataloging-in-Publication Data

Fitzgerald, Theresa.
 Math dictionary for kids : the essential guide to math, terms, strategies, and tables : grades 4-9 /
by Theresa R. Fitzgerald.
    p. cm.
 Includes index.
 ISBN 978-1-59363-644-9 (pbk.)
 1. Mathematics--Dictionaries, Juvenile. 2. Mathematics--Handbooks, manuals, etc.--Juvenile
literature. I. Title.
 QA5.F58 2011
 510.3--dc23
                                     2011019284

Edited by Jennifer Robins

Layout design by Raquel Trevino

ISBN-13: 978-1-59363-644-9

Printed in the United States of America.

PO10311 05162011 BP312379

At the time of this book's publication, all facts and figures cited are the most current available.
All telephone numbers, addresses, and website URLs are accurate and active. All publications,
organizations, websites, and other resources exist as described in the book, and all have been
verified. The author and Prufrock Press Inc. make no warranty or guarantee concerning the information and materials given out by organizations or content found at websites, and we are not
responsible for any changes that occur after this book's publication. If you find an error, please
contact Prufrock Press Inc.

Prufrock Press Inc.
P.O. Box 8813
Waco, TX 76714-8813
Phone: (800) 998-2208
Fax: (800) 240-0333
http://www.prufrock.com

With many thanks to
John Fitzgerald, Rebecca McCormick,
and Sheliah Shepard

Dedicated with love to:

John Joel Fitzgerald, my husband,
and Amanda Therese Fitzgerald, our daughter
(December 5, 1981–March 31, 2002)

Table of Contents

Introduction

E very discipline has its own unique vocabulary, a group of words and definitions that people use to study or communicate information within that field. The key to understanding any subject is knowing its terminology. Likewise, mathematics has a vocabulary, consisting of words and symbols, that allows people to have a common base of understanding. And, like other disciplines, knowing the vocabulary of mathematics gives one the power to unlock problems.

There are many keys to being a proficient math problem solver, and two of the most important elements to successful problem solving are knowing:

- what the problem is asking (understanding the vocabulary and being able to determine which strategy to employ), and
- how to perform the operation(s) (being able to quickly and automatically perform the necessary operations).

Besides providing information that will help math students in these two important areas of problem solving, this math dictionary also offers a wealth of other information, compiled in an easy-to-use format.

The *Math Dictionary for Kids* is much more than a compilation of words and definitions. This book has been organized to reflect the different areas of mathematics taught in elementary and junior high schools. Each category includes the terms commonly used in this field of study, concise definitions, and many examples and illustrations. In addition, the book provides quick reference guides for basic operations and tables of commonly used facts and equivalents.

This is a book that should be used throughout the year. It can be used on a daily basis in the whole-class setting to review the vocabulary and operations associated with the math unit being studied. This daily review provides continuous reinforcement that leads to proficiency. The book can also be used on an individual basis. A student can take it out of his or her desk as a reference to check what a term means or how an operation is performed. This cuts down on the chances of making mistakes, aids comprehension, and builds self-reliance.

Once you use a reference like this book, you'll agree that it truly is absolutely essential. It will be the reference material you will use again and again to supplement and reinforce each topic in your mathematics curriculum.

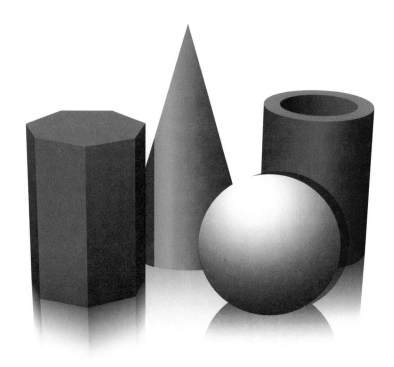

Whole Numbers and Operations

Addends

Numbers in addition problems that are added together to form a sum.

Example:
3 + 7 = 10
3 and 7 are addends.

Addition

The process of uniting two or more numbers into a sum; counting the total.
Key word: altogether

Examples:
☺☺☺ + ☺☺ = ☺☺☺☺☺
3 + 2 = 5

Arabic Numbers

A Base-10 place-value number system that uses the symbols 0, 1, 2, 3, 4, 5, 6, 7, 8, and 9. Also called Hindu-Arabic numbers.

Arithmetic Progression

A series of numbers in which each number differs from the preceding number by a fixed amount. A series of numbers that follows a pattern.

Example:
1, 5, 9, 13, 17, 21, 25, 29, . . .
Each number differs by 4.

Ascend

To increase in number, value, or amount.

Ascending Order

Increasing from least to greatest, but not necessarily according to a fixed pattern. To count upward from smallest to largest; counting up.

Examples:
35, 37, 39, 41, 43, 45, 47, 49, . . .
An example of an ascending arithmetic progression.

1, 5, 13, 40, 53
A series of numbers in ascending order.

Whole Numbers and Operations

Binary Numbers

A numerical system that is based on the number 2. Each place has a value equal to a power of 2, as indicated or shown by the symbols 0 or 1.

Base 10	1	2	3	4	5	6	7	8	9
Base 2	1	10	11	100	101	110	111	1000	1001

Cardinal Numbers

Numbers used for counting or answering the question "how many?"; they show quantity.
Key words: counting numbers

Example:
Numbers such as 1, 2, 3, 47, and 104 are cardinal numbers.

Common Factor/Common Divisor

A factor that two or more numbers have in common. A number that divides two or more numbers evenly (without a remainder).

Example 1:
When using tiles to look at two numbers, the common factors are the factors that both numbers share.

To build the number 6, the numerals 1, 2, 3, and 6 are used.

To build the number 8, the numerals 1, 2, 4, and 8 are used.

The factors that 6 and 8 have in common, or share, are 1 and 2.

Example 2:

①② 3, and 6 are the factors of 6.
①② 4, and 8 are the factors of 8.

The factors that 6 and 8 have in common, or share, are 1 and 2.

Math Dictionary for Kids

Common Multiple

Any number that is a multiple of two or more numbers; a multiple that two or more numbers have in common, or share.

Key words: common, shared

Example:

Multiples of 2	2	4	6	8	10	12	14	16	18	. . .
Multiples of 3	3	6	9	12	15	18	21	24	27	. . .
Multiples of 4	4	8	12	16	20	24	28	32	36	. . .
Multiples of 5	5	10	15	20	25	30	35	40	45	. . .
Multiples of 6	6	12	18	24	30	36	42	48	54	. . .

12 is a common multiple of 2, 3, 4, and 6.

Composing Numbers

The process of creating a larger number through addition.

Example:
1,000 + 300 + 10 + 7 is composed as 1,317.

Composite Number

A number that has factors other than 1 and itself. A number that can be built in more than one way using tiles. Composite numbers can be written as the product of prime numbers.

Example:

The number **6** is composite because there is more than one way to build it.

Other examples:

9 = 1 × 9 or 3 × 3

90 = 2 × 5 × 9

40 = 2 × 2 × 2 × 5

Counting Numbers

The positive whole numbers. Also called natural numbers.

Example:
1, 2, 3, 4, 5, . . .

Decline

To decrease in number, value, or amount.

Decomposing Numbers

The process of separating a number into its component parts.

Example:
3,487 can be decomposed as
3,000 + 400 + 80 + 7.

Decrease

To make less (smaller).

Descending Order

Decreasing from greatest to least, but not necessarily in a fixed pattern. To count downward from largest to smallest.

Example:
101, 90, 87, 72, 56
A series of numbers in descending order.

Difference

The answer to a subtraction problem.

Example:
7 – 5 = 2
2 is the difference between the numbers.

Dividend

The number in division that is to be divided, or broken, into equal parts.

Example:

$$6\overline{)30}^{5} \text{ or } 30 \div 5 = 6$$

30 is the dividend.

Divisibility Rules

2   A number is divisible by 2 if it is even or if the last digit is divisible by 2.

3   A number is divisible by 3 if the sum of its digits is divisible by 3.

4   A number is divisible by 4 if the number formed by the last two digits is divisible by 4 or if the last two digits are two zeros.

5   A number is divisible by 5 if its last digit is 5 or zero.

6   A number is divisible by 6 if the number is even and is divisible by 3.

Divisibility Rules, continued

9 A number is divisible by 9 if the sum of its digits is divisible by 9.

10 A number is divisible by 10 if its last digit is a zero.

Divisible

Capable of being divided evenly without leaving a remainder.

Example:
$20 \div 4 = 5$
20 is divisible by 4.

Division

The process of division, meaning:

1. Breaking a number into smaller groups of equal quantities.
2. Repeated subtraction; subtracting the same number again and again.
3. Breaking a number into an equal amount of same-sized pieces.

Key words: evenly divided, evenly split, evenly shared between or among, fair shares, even groups of, how many would each get . . ., divisor, dividend, quotient, remainder, left over, fraction

Example:

$$4\overline{)12}^{\,3}$$

4 is the divisor, 12 is the dividend, and 3 is the quotient.

Division Strategies

✪ Larger Numbers: Multiples Table

1. Make a multiples table (see p. 8) for the number you are dividing by, the divisor.
2. Subtract the largest multiple of the divisor that does not exceed the dividend.
3. When you can't subtract any more multiples of 100s, begin subtracting multiples of 10s, and then multiples of 1 through 9.
4. When you can't subtract any more multiples, add the number of multiples that have been subtracted. This final number is the quotient.

Division Strategies, continued

✪ Larger Numbers: Multiples Table, continued

Multiples Table for 34

1	34	11	374
2	68	20	680
3	102	30	1,020
4	136	40	1,360
5	170	50	1,700
6	204	60	2,040
7	238	70	2,380
8	272	80	2,720
9	306	90	3,060
10	340	100	3,400

$$
\begin{array}{r}
100+80+3 \\
34\overline{)6243} \\
-3400 \\
\hline
2843 \\
-2720 \\
\hline
123 \\
-102 \\
\hline
21
\end{array}
$$

Answer: 183 r 21

✪ **Repeated Subtraction**

23 was subtracted a total of four imes with 6 remaining, so the answer is **4 r 6** or **4 $\frac{6}{23}$**.

$$
\begin{array}{r}
4\frac{6}{23} \text{ or } 4 \text{ r } 6 \\
23\overline{)98} \\
-23 \\
\hline
75 \\
-23 \\
\hline
52 \\
-23 \\
\hline
29 \\
-23 \\
\hline
6
\end{array}
$$

Division Strategies, continued

✪ Use Manipulatives

Use beans, counters, or other objects, or draw a picture. Count out the number of beans that need to be divided. Divide them equally into the number of groups that are you are dividing by.

$43 \div 6 = 7 \text{ r } 1$

Use tiles or paper squares. Count out the number of tiles that need to be divided. Put them into the number of rows you are dividing by. Count the number of columns you make, and then count the remainder.

$13 \div 5 = 2 \text{ r } 3$

Divisor

The number in a division problem by which the dividend is divided. The number used to divide by.

Example:

$$4\overline{)28}^{\,7}$$

or $28 \div 4 = 7$ **4** is the divisor.

Double

To count something twice.
Twice as much.

Example:
Double 3 means the same thing as
$3 + 3 = 6$ or $3 \times 2 = 6$.

Equality

The property of being equal. The following are true of equal numbers:

- $a = a$
- If $a = b$, then $b = a$
- If $a = b$ and $b = c$, then $a = c$

Even Number

A whole number that has 0, 2, 4, 6, or 8 in the ones place. It can be divided evenly into two equal groups with no remainder. Even numbers are divisible by 2.

Example:
14 is an even number; when put into two equal groups, there is no remainder.

Expanded Form

Numbers broken up into their individual place values.

Example:
$$3{,}422 = 3{,}000 + 400 + 20 + 2$$
$$= (3 \times 1{,}000) + (4 \times 100) + (2 \times 10) + 2$$
$$= (3 \times 10^3) + (4 \times 10^2) + (2 \times 10^1) + (2 \times 10^0)$$

Fact Family

A group of addition and subtraction or multiplication and division facts made from the same three numbers.

Examples:
Addition/Subtraction (3, 7, 10)

$7 + 3 = 10$	$10 - 3 = 7$
$3 + 7 = 10$	$10 - 7 = 3$

Multiplication/Division (3, 8, 24)

$3 \times 8 = 24$	$24 \div 8 = 3$
$8 \times 3 = 24$	$24 \div 3 = 8$

Factor

One of two or more numbers that are multiplied together to get a product (the answer).

Example:
6 x 7 = 42
6 and **7** are factors of 42.

Factorial

The product of consecutive numbers, always starting with the number 1. It is symbolized by using an exclamation point (!).

Examples:
3! = 1 x 2 x 3 = 6
6! = 1 x 2 x 3 x 4 x 5 x 6 = 720

Greater Than/Less Than

A way of comparing two groups of objects using the symbols > and <. The symbols for greater than and less than can be remembered in these ways:

Two are greater than one. The side with two ends points toward the larger number.

Mouths with sharp teeth like to take bigger bites!

Example: 8 < 11

Greatest Common Factor

The largest number that is a common factor, or divisor, of two numbers.

Example:
Factors of 30: **1**, **2**, **3**, 5, **6**, 10, 15, 30
Factors of 24: **1**, **2**, **3**, 4, **6**, 8, 12, 24
1, **2**, **3**, and **6** are the common factors of 24 and 30. The greatest common factor is 6.

Hindu-Arabic Numbers

A Base-10 place-value number system that uses the symbols 0, 1, 2, 3, 4, 5, 6, 7, 8, and 9. Also called Arabic numbers.

Increase

To make more (larger).

Infinite

Having so many that the quantity is unable to be measured or counted. The symbol for infinity is ∞. Infinite sets are also noted with the symbol . . . , which means that the numbers go on and on forever.

Example:
2, 4, 6, 8, 10, 12, . . .

Integer

Another way to name whole numbers and zero. Integers can be either positive or negative, but they do not include fractions, mixed numbers, or decimals.

Examples:
0, 5, 17, and 487
Examples of positive integers.

-334, -15, -3, and -1
Examples of negative integers.

½, 3¼, and .09 are not examples of integers because they are not whole numbers.

Inverse Operation

The opposite operation. Subtraction is the inverse of addition, and division is the inverse of multiplication.

Irrational Numbers

Numbers that can be written as decimals but not as fractions. These decimals do not repeat or terminate.

Examples:
The square root of 2 = $\sqrt{2}$ = 1.41421 . . .
The square root of 3 = $\sqrt{3}$ = 1.73205 . . .
pi (π) = 3.14159 . . .

Laws of Arithmetic

There are several laws that govern basic arithmetic operations.

✪ Associative Law (Grouping Property)

Changing the way the addends or factors are grouped does not change the sum or the product.

Examples:

Addition	Multiplication
(a + b) + c = a + (b + c)	(a x b) x c = a x (b x c)
(4 + 9) + 1 = 4 + (9 + 1)	(2 x 5) x 10 = 2 x (5 x 10)

✪ Commutative Law (Order Property)

Changing the order of the addends does not change the sum or product.

Examples:

Addition	Multiplication
a + b = b + a	a x b = b x a
7 + 12 = 12 + 7	3 x 8 = 8 x 3

✪ Distributive Law

A number that is multiplied by the sum of two or more numbers is the same as the sum of that number multiplied by each of the numbers separately.

Example:

a x (b + c) = (a x b) + (a x c)

2 x (3 + 4) = (2 x 3) + (2 x 4)

✪ Zero Property of Addition

Any number plus zero equals that number.

Example:

467 + 0 = 467

-8 + 0 = -8

✪ Zero Property of Multiplication

Any number multiplied by zero equals zero.

Examples:

7 x 0 = 0

0 x 33 = 0

-5 x 0 = 0

Less Than/Greater Than

See *Greater Than/Less Than*

Lowest Common Multiple (LCM)

The lowest multiple that two or more numbers have in common.

Example:
Multiples of 2: 2 4 **6** 8 10 **12** 14 16 **18** 20 22 **24** . . .
Multiples of 3: 3 **6** 9 **12** 15 **18** 21 **24** 27 30 33 36 . . .

6, 12, 18, and **24** are all multiples of 2 and 3, but 6 is the lowest common multiple because it is the first number that is in both sets.

Minuend

A number from which another number is subtracted.

Example:
23 – 5 = 18
23 is the minuend.

Multiple

A number that is the product of a specific number and another whole number. The numbers said when counting by the same number repeatedly.

Examples:
2 x 6 = 12
12 is a multiple of 2 and 6.

Count by 3:
3, 6, 9, 12, 15, 18, 21, . . .
The numbers are multiples of 3.

MULTIPLES OF	1	2	3	4	5	6	7	8	9
1	1	2	3	4	5	6	7	8	9
2	2	4	6	8	10	12	14	16	18
3	3	6	9	12	15	18	21	24	27
4	4	8	12	16	20	24	28	32	36
5	5	10	15	20	25	30	35	40	45
6	6	12	18	24	30	36	42	48	54
7	7	14	21	28	35	42	49	56	63
8	8	16	24	32	40	48	56	64	72
9	9	18	27	36	45	54	63	72	81

Multiplication

Repeated addition. Adding the same number a given number of times.

Key words: total, in all, altogether, _____ groups of _____, area, product, factor, multiples, square, prime, composite, square root

Example:
$4 \times 3 = 12$ is the same as
$3 + 3 + 3 + 3 = 12$.
They are both four groups of 3.

Multiplication Strategies

✪ Break Apart

Example:
$4 \times 6 =$ $2 \times 6 = 12$
            $2 \times 6 = 12$
            $12 + 12 = 24$

✪ Break Apart (Larger Numbers)

Example:

$$
\begin{array}{cc}
47 \\
\times\ 6
\end{array}
\longrightarrow
\begin{array}{cc}
40 \\
\times\ 6 \\
\hline
240
\end{array}
\ +\
\begin{array}{cc}
7 \\
\times\ 6 \\
\hline
42
\end{array}
$$

$240 + 42 = 282$

✪ "Count By" Using Multiples

Example:
$6 + 6 + 6 + 6 = 24$
     or
6   12   18   24

✪ Crossed Lines (Count Intersections)

Example:

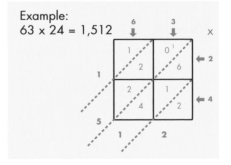

✪ Draw a Picture

Example

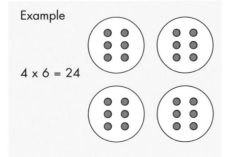

$4 \times 6 = 24$

✪ Window Pane Math

Example:
$63 \times 24 = 1,512$

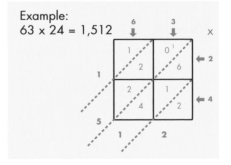

Numbers, Sets of

Natural or counting numbers $\{1, 2, 3, 4, 5, 6, \ldots\}$

Whole numbers $\{0, 1, 2, 3, 4, 5, 6, \ldots\}$

Integers $\{\ldots, -4, -3, -2, -1, 0, 1, 2, 3, 4, \ldots\}$

Negative integers $\{\ldots, -7, -6, -5, -4, -3, -2, -1\}$

Positive integers $\{1, 2, 3, 4, 5, 6, 7, 8, \ldots\}$

Rational numbers   the set of integers, as well as numbers that can be written as proper and improper fractions

Irrational numbers   the set of numbers that can be written as decimals but not as fractions

Numeral

A word or symbol used to represent a number.

Example:
The numeral 7 represents seven things.

Odd Number

A whole number that has a 1, 3, 5, 7, or 9 in the ones place. When divided into two groups, there will be a remainder.

Example:
15 is an odd number; when put into two equal groups, there is a remainder.

Order of Operations

A set of rules agreed upon by mathematicians that outline the steps to take when solving multioperational problems. These rules help reduce confusion when solving problems and ensure that the same answer can be reached every time.

Order of Operations, continued

Sometimes it helps to remember PEMDAS. "**P**lease **E**xcuse **M**y **D**ear **A**unt **S**ally" stands for:

1. Complete the work in **parentheses** (or brackets) first.
2. Simplify **exponents**.
3. **Multiply** or **divide** from left to right.
4. **Add** or **subtract** from left to right.

Example:
$6^2 + 15 \times (1 + 3) \div 5 =$
$6^2 + 15 \times 4 \div 5 =$
$36 + 15 \times 4 \div 5 =$
$36 + 60 \div 5 =$
$36 + 12 = 48$

Sometimes problems may not have all of the components listed above (parentheses, exponents, multiplication/division, and addition/subtraction). If so, continue down the list of steps until you reach a step that fits the problem.

Example:
$9 - 3 + 2 \times 6 =$ There are no parentheses or exponents,
$9 - 3 + 12 =$ so begin with Step 3 of PEMDAS.
$6 + 12 = 18$

Ordinal Numbers

Numbers that express degree, quality, or position. Numerals that show order.

Example:
First, second, third   Examples of ordinal numbers.
1, 2, 3   Examples of cardinal numbers.

Pair

A set or sets of two. Two of a kind.

= 1 pair   = 3 pairs   = 3 pairs with one left over

Periods

A way to name the groups of three numbers that make up place value.

Trillions Period	Billions Period	Millions Period	Thousands Period	Units (Ones) Period
— — —	, — — —	, — — —	, — — —	, — — —

Place Value

The value given to the space a digit holds because of its place in a numeral. These values are named according to the spot each takes up.

Example:

hundred billions	ten billions	billions	hundred millions	ten millions	millions	hundred thousands	ten thousands	thousands	hundreds	tens	ones	AND	tenths	hundredths	thousandths	ten thousandths
1	4	7	6	8	5	9	3	6	0	2	1	.	4	7	6	3

Prime Factors

Prime numbers that, when multiplied, will result in a given number. Use division to find the prime factors of a number.

Example:
The prime factors of the number 16 are circled.

16 can be divided by 2 evenly. Two is a prime number, but 8 can be divided again.

4 can be divided further.

The **prime factors** of 16 are **2, 2, 2,** and **2**.

16 = 2 x 2 x 2 x 2

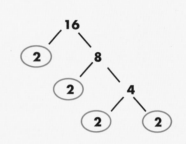

Example:
The prime factors of the number 27 are circled.

The **prime factors** of 27 are **3, 3,** and **3**.

27 = 3 x 3 x 3

Example:
The prime factors of the number 10 are circled.

The **prime factors** of 10 are **2** and **5**.

10 = 2 x 5

Prime Number

A whole number greater than 1 that has only itself and the number 1 as factors. A number that can be built only one way using tiles. The first 10 prime numbers are 2, 3, 5, 7, 11, 13, 17, 19, 23, and 29.

Math Dictionary for Kids

Prime Number, continued

Example:
17 is a prime number because:
- it can only be built using 1 row of 17 tiles,
- 1 x 17 = 17, and
- its only factors are 1 and 17.

17

1

$1 \times 17 = 17$

Product

The answer to a multiplication problem.

Example:
$4 \times 8 = 32$ **32** is the product.

Progression

A sequence of numbers that has a fixed pattern.

✪ Arithmetic Progression

Each term is the result of adding or subtracting a given number.

Example:
3, 7, 11, 15, 19, . . .
Each number increases by **4** in this arithmetic progression.

✪ Geometric Progression

Each term is obtained by multiplying the preceding term by a given number.

Example:
1, 3, 9, 27, 81, . . .
Each number is multiplied by **3** in this geometric progression.

Quotient

The number that is the answer to a division problem, not including the remainder.

Example:

```
    7 r 3
6 ) 45
   -42
     3
```

$45 \div 6 = 7 \text{ r } 3$ **7** is the quotient.

Rational Numbers

Numbers that can be written as a ratio. They can be named as fractions or as decimals. These include integers (3, 23), fractions ($\frac{1}{4}$, $\frac{1}{100}$), and terminating or repeating decimals (.25, .333 . . .).

Examples:
.978   .323232
57   1.25 (which equals $\frac{5}{4}$)
-6 $\frac{1}{2}$

Relationship Symbols

Symbols used to compare the values of two or more numbers or expressions. The most commonly used are =, ≠, >, and <, but there are many more. Also see *Symbols*.

Remainder

The number smaller than the divisor that is left over after the division process has been completed. What is left over after you have put all that you can into equal groups.

Example:
10 ÷ 3 = 3 r 1   1 is the remainder.

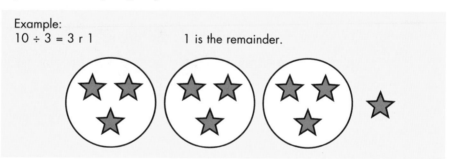

Roman Numerals

Roman letters used to represent numbers. These are usually written in capitals, but they can also be written in lowercase letters. The number is multiplied by 1,000 if there is a bar, or line, over the letter(s).

1 = I	10 = X	19 = XIX
2 = II	11 = XI	20 = XX
3 = III	12 = XII	50 = L
4 = IV	13 = XIII	100 = C
5 = V	14 = XIV	500 = D
6 = VI	15 = XV	1,000 = M
7 = VII	16 = XVI	15,000 = $\overline{XV}$
8 = VIII	17 = XVII	
9 = IX	18 = XVIII	

Whole Numbers and Operations

Sequence

A set of numbers that is arranged so that there is a pattern. Usually written with the numbers separated by commas.

Example:
2, 7, 4, 9, 6, 11, 8, . . .

Square

To multiply a number by itself.

Example:
$4^2 = 4 \times 4 = 16$

Square Number

A number measured in two dimensions, length and width. To multiply a number by itself. Square numbers are shown with a small 2 above and to the right of the number or unit. Naturally square numbers form a perfect square when built with tiles.

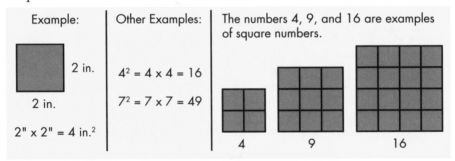

Example:

2 in.

2 in.

2" x 2" = 4 in.²

Other Examples:

$4^2 = 4 \times 4 = 16$

$7^2 = 7 \times 7 = 49$

The numbers 4, 9, and 16 are examples of square numbers.

4   9   16

Square Root

A number that, when squared (multiplied by itself), will produce a given number. The symbol for square root is $\sqrt{\ }$.

★ $\sqrt{49}$ = +7 or -7
   The square root of 49 is +7 or -7.
★ The principal square root is the positive square root.
   $\sqrt{36} = 6$ $\sqrt{100} = 10$

Square Root, continued

Example:
The square root of 9 is 3.

	3		
3	1	2	3
	4	5	6
	7	8	9

Standard Form

Numbers written in regular number form.

Example:
Three thousand four hundred twenty-two would be written as 3,422.

Subtraction

The process of finding the difference between two numbers.

Subtrahend

The number that is subtracted.

Example:
$9 - 6 = 3$ **6** is the subtrahend.

Sum

The answer to an addition problem.

Example:
$4 + 5 = 9$ **9** is the sum.

Triple

To triple a number. Three times as much.

Example:
Triple 4 means the same thing as
$4 + 4 + 4 = 12$ or $4 \times 3 = 12$

Twice as Much

Two times as much or two times as many.

Example:
Twice as much as 6 means the same as $6 + 6 = 12$ or $6 \times 2 = 12$

Whole Numbers and Operations

Whole Number

A number without a fraction or decimal part.

Examples:
1, 34, and 256 are whole numbers.
½, 5 ¹³⁄₂₂, .45, and 3.7 are not whole numbers.

Zero

The numeral indicating none.

Measurement

Area

The measurement surface of a region in square units. To find the area, count the squares that can fit inside the object, or multiply the length by the width.

Example:

1 square unit

2 units

3 units

Area = 2 units x 3 units = 6 square units

Capacity

The volume of a figure, or the amount of space an object fills. How much something will hold.

Celsius

See *Temperature.*

Centimeter

A unit of metric measurement used to measure length; one centimeter equals 1/100th of a meter; abbreviated cm; also spelled centimetre. One centimeter is about as wide as your little finger is across. See *Metric Measurement–Length.*

Cubed

Having the same measurement in length, width, and height. To raise a number to the third power.

Cubic

Having three dimensions. A cubic solid will have length, width, and height, like a block. Cubic measurements are shown with a small 3 above and to the right of the unit abbreviation.

Example:
Volume = 4^3= 4 x 4 x 4, so
4^3 = 64 in.

4 in.→

4 in.

4 in.

Cup

A unit of standard measurement used to measure capacity, or volume; often used in cooking; abbreviated c. See *Standard Measurement–Capacity*.

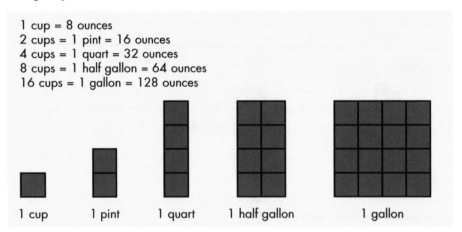

1 cup = 8 ounces
2 cups = 1 pint = 16 ounces
4 cups = 1 quart = 32 ounces
8 cups = 1 half gallon = 64 ounces
16 cups = 1 gallon = 128 ounces

1 cup   1 pint   1 quart   1 half gallon   1 gallon

Decimeter

A unit of metric measurement used to measure length; one decimeter equals 1/10th of a meter; abbreviated dm; also spelled decimetre. One decimeter is a little wider than the width of the widest part of your hand. See *Metric Measurement–Length*.

Degree

A unit of measure for angles. A circle is divided into 360 degrees.

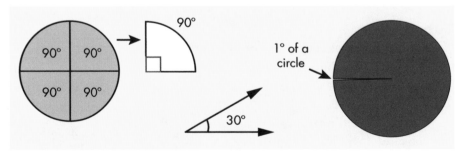

90°
90° 90°
90° 90°

90°

1° of a circle

30°

Dimension

Measurement in length, width, depth, or height. The size of something.

Measurement

Distance

The length of a straight line between two points. How far it is from one point to another.

Estimate

To find an answer that is close to the exact answer. Your best guess.

Fahrenheit

See *Temperature*.

Foot

A unit of standard measurement used to measure length; 1 foot equals 12 inches; abbreviated ft. See *Standard Measurement–Length*.

Gallon

A unit of standard measurement used to measure capacity, or volume; there are 128 fluid ounces in a gallon; abbreviated gal. See *Standard Measurement–Weight*.

Gram

A unit of metric measurement used to measure weight; abbreviated g. One gram weighs about as much as a standard paper clip, or about as much as a unit cube of Base-10 blocks. See *Metric Measurement–Weight*.

Half Gallon

A unit of standard measurement used to measure capacity, or volume; there are 64 fluid ounces in a half gallon. See *Standard Measurement–Capacity*.

Inch

A unit of standard measurement used to measure length; abbreviated in. One inch is about the width of a quarter. See *Standard Measurement–Length*.

Kilogram

A unit of metric measurement used to measure weight; abbreviated kg. See *Metric Measurement–Weight*.

Kiloliter

A unit of metric measurement used to measure capacity; abbreviated kl; also spelled kilolitre. See *Metric Measurement–Capacity*.

Kilometer

A unit of metric measurement used to measure length; abbreviated km; also spelled kilometre. See *Metric Measurement–Length*.

Length

One-dimensional measurement. The distance from one end to the other end of a line segment. How long something is. When trying to decide which measurement is the length and which is the width, remember that *length* is usually the *longer* of the two.

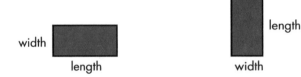

Liter

A unit of metric measurement used to measure capacity; abbreviated L; also spelled litre. See *Metric Measurement–Capacity*.

Measurement

The size or dimension of something determined by measuring.

✪ Metric Measurement
Capacity (Volume):

milliliter (ml)	one centicube is a milliliter	1,000 milliliters = 1 liter
liter (L)	1 liter = 1,000 milliliters	
kiloliter (kl)	1 kiloliter = 1,000 liters	

Measurement, continued
✪ Metric Measurement, continued

Length:

millimeter (mm)	*about as thick as the skinny part of a dime* 10 millimeters = 1 centimeter
centimeter (cm)	*about as wide as your little finger is across* 10 centimeters = 1 decimeter 100 centimeters = 1 meter

View of expanded size metric ruler: 1 centimeter
The little lines in between the "cm" and the "1"
are millimeters.

decimeter (dm)	1 decimeter = 10 centimeters 10 decimeters = 1 meter
meter (m)	1 meter = 10 dm = 100 cm = 1,000 mm
kilometer (km)	*used to measure long distances* 1 kilometer = 1,000 meters

Weight:

milligram (mg)	1,000 milligrams = 1 gram
gram (g)	*about the mass of a paper clip, or one centicube* 1 gram = 1,000 milligrams 1,000 grams = 1 kilogram
kilogram (kg)	1 kilogram = 1,000 grams

Measurement, continued
✪ Standard Measurement
Capacity (Volume):

cup (c)	1 cup = 8 ounces
	2 cups = 1 pint = 16 ounces
	4 cups = 1 quart = 32 ounces
pint (pt)	2 pints = 1 quart = 32 ounces
quart (qt)	4 quarts = 1 gallon = 128 ounces
half gallon	1 half gallon = 2 quarts = 64 ounces
gallon (gal)	1 gallon = 4 quarts = 128 ounces

Length:

inch (in. or ")	*about as wide as a quarter*	12 inches = 1 foot
foot (ft or ')	1 foot = 12 inches	
	3 feet = 36 inches = 1 yard	
yard (yd)	1 yard = 3 feet = 36 inches	
mile (mi)	1 mile = 5,280 feet	

View of expanded size standard ruler: 1 inch

Weight:

ounce (oz)	16 ounces = 1 pound
pound (lb)	1 pound = 16 ounces
ton (T)	1 ton = 2,000 pounds

Meter

A unit of metric measurement used to measure length; abbreviated m; also spelled metre. See *Metric Measurement–Length*.

Mile

A unit of standard measurement used to measure length; abbreviated mi. See *Standard Measurement–Length*.

Milligram

A unit of standard measurement used to measure weight; abbreviated mg. See *Metric Measurement–Weight*.

Milliliter

A unit of metric measurement used to measure capacity; abbreviated ml; also spelled millilitre. See *Metric Measurement–Capacity*.

Millimeter

A unit of metric measurement used to measure length; abbreviated mm; also spelled millimetre. See *Metric Measurement–Length*.

Money

The standard measure of exchange that is used to buy goods and services, with each unit having a value. The denominations of money used in the United States and Canada are given below.

✪ Penny (coin in U.S. and Canada)

A penny equals one cent.
It takes 100 pennies to make $1.

```
1 penny = 1 cent (.01¢)
5 pennies = 1 nickel (.05¢)
10 pennies = 1 dime (.10¢)
25 pennies = 1 quarter (.25¢)
50 pennies = 1 half-dollar (.50¢)
100 pennies = 1 dollar ($1.00)
```

✪ Nickel (coin in U.S. and Canada)

One nickel equals five cents.

```
1 nickel = 5 cents (.05¢)
2 nickels = 1 dime (.10¢)
5 nickels = 1 quarter (.25¢)
20 nickels = 1 dollar ($1.00)
```

Measurement

Money, continued

✪ Dime (coin in U.S. and Canada)
One dime equals 10 cents.

1 dime = 10 cents (.10¢)
5 dimes = 50 cents = 2 quarters (.50¢)
10 dimes = 1 dollar ($1)

✪ Quarter (coin in U.S. and Canada)
One quarter equals 25 cents.

1 quarter = 25 cents (.25¢)
2 quarters = 50 cents (.50¢)
4 quarters = 1 dollar ($1)

✪ Half-Dollar (coin in U.S.)
One half-dollar equals 50 cents.

1 half-dollar = 50 cents (.50¢)
2 half-dollars = 1 dollar ($1)

✪ Dollar (paper currency in U.S., coin in Canada)
One dollar equals 100 cents. In the United States, the dollar bill is paper currency; in Canada, the dollar is a coin commonly called a Loonie, in reference to the Loon minted on it. Although the United States has a $2 bill, it is no longer commonly used and is rare to see one in circulation. A $2 coin in Canada called a Toonie is in active circulation.

Money, continued
✪ Dollar, continued

1 dollar = 2 half-dollars
        = 4 quarters
        = 10 dimes
        = 20 nickels
        = 100 pennies

$1 Loonie, Canada

$2 Toonie, Canada

Measurement

Ounce
A unit of standard measurement used to measure weight; abbreviated oz. See *Standard Measurement–Weight*.

Perimeter
The distance around the outside of a figure. To find the perimeter of a rectangular or square figure, find the measurement of each side of the object, and then add the numbers together.

3 units

2 units   2 units   perimeter = 2 + 3 + 2 + 3 = 10 units

3 units

Pint
A unit of standard measurement used to measure capacity; abbreviated pt. See *Standard Measurement–Capacity*.

Pound
A unit of standard measurement used to measure weight; there are 16 ounces in a pound; abbreviated lb. See *Standard Measurement–Weight*.

Protractor

An instrument in the shape of a semicircle used for drawing and measuring angles in degrees.

Quart

A unit of standard measurement used to measure capacity; abbreviated qt. See *Standard Measurement–Capacity*.

Rounding

Rewriting a number as its nearest multiple of 10, 100, 1,000, and so on. If the number to the right of the place you are rounding to is 0–4, the number stays the same. If it is 5–9, the number rounds up to the next greater number. The rest of the numbers to the right of the original number become zeros.

Example 1:
Round **3,294** to the nearest thousand.

Look at the number in the place you are rounding; underline it and the number right after it. **3,294**

The number to the right of the 3 is 2, so the 3 will stay the same. The rest of the numbers will change to zeros. Therefore, 3,294 rounds to **3,000** when rounding to the nearest thousand.

Example 2:
Round to the nearest 10

566	⟶	570
562	⟶	560
3,049	⟶	3,050

Rounding, continued

Round to the nearest 100

<u>5</u>66 ⟶	600
<u>5</u>36 ⟶	500
76,<u>8</u>24 ⟶	76,800

Round to the nearest 10,000

<u>6</u>4,340 ⟶	60,000
8<u>6</u>8,473 ⟶	870,000
4<u>0</u>6,299 ⟶	410,000

Ruler

A tool used for measuring and drawing straight lines that is usually divided into units and fractional parts of the units, such as inches or centimeters.

Scale

Any instrument that is divided into equal units that can be used to measure. Rulers, thermometers, and weighing devices are examples of scales. Weighing devices are most commonly referred to as scales or balance scales.

Squared

Measuring in two dimensions. A squared figure will be measured for length and width, like a square. Squared measurements are shown with a small 2 above and to the right of the unit abbreviation.

Example:

5"

5"

Volume = 5^2 = 5 x 5, so 5^2 = 25 in.

Measurement

35

Measurement

Surface Area

The combined areas of all surfaces of a three-dimensional figure.

Example 1:
One face of a cube is 3 x 3, which equals 9. There are 6 faces on a cube, so 9 x 6 = 54.

Example 2:
The surface area of a cube with sides equal to 4 is 6 x 4^2, so 6 x 16 = 96.

Temperature

The measure of hotness or coldness of an object.

✪ Celsius

Metric, or centigrade, scale of measurement of temperature that is abbreviated with a capital C.

0° C = freezing point of water
100° C = boiling point of water
20° C = normal room temperature

✪ Fahrenheit

Standard scale of measurement of temperature that is abbreviated with a capital F.

32° F = freezing point of water
212° F = boiling point of water
70° F = normal room temperature

Thermometer

An instrument used for measuring temperatures in Celsius, Fahrenheit, or both.

Time

A number that represents a specific interval such as hours, days, or years.

a.m.   The time from 12:00 midnight to noon.
p.m.   The time from 12:00 noon to midnight.

60 seconds = 1 minute
60 minutes = 1 hour
24 hours = 1 day
7 days = 1 week
365 or 366 days = 1 year

52 weeks = 1 year
10 years = 1 decade
10 decades = 1 century
100 years = 1 century
1,000 years = 1 millennium

Time, continued

There are 12 months in each year, each with a set number of days:

Months in the Year	Days in Each Month
January	31
February	28 (29 in leap years)
March	31
April	30
May	31
June	30
July	31
August	31
September	30
October	31
November	30
December	31

Measurement

Ton

A unit of standard measurement used to measure weight; abbreviated T. See *Standard Measurement–Weight*.

Unit

A standard of measurement such as millimeters, centimeters, inches, feet, meters, yards, miles, ounces, grams, or pounds. Any amount used as a standard for measuring area, length, or volume.

Volume

The amount of space, measured in cubic units, that something takes up. Finding the volume of a space (three-dimensional) figure is often calculated using multiplication. See the formulas on page 38.

Measurement

Volume, continued

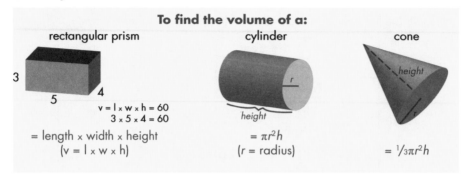

To find the volume of a:

rectangular prism

3
5
4
$v = l \times w \times h = 60$
$3 \times 5 \times 4 = 60$
= length x width x height
$(v = l \times w \times h)$

cylinder

r
height
$= \pi r^2 h$
$(r = \text{radius})$

cone

height
r
$= \frac{1}{3}\pi r^2 h$

Weight

The gravitational pull on an object. The measure of the heaviness of an object. Common units of measure are ounce, pound, gram, kilogram, and ton.

Width

The distance from one side of an object to the other side. How wide something is.

Yard

A unit of standard measurement used to measure length; abbreviated yd. See *Standard Measurement–Length.*

Algebraic Ideas

Absolute Value

The value of a number regardless of its sign, denoted by the numeral between two parallel lines. The distance from the origin to that number on a number line.

Example:
$|+3| = 3$ and $|-3| = 3$

Abundant Number

A number in which the sum of its factors is larger than two times the number.

Example:
$12 = 1, 2, 3, 4, 6, 12$
$1 + 2 + 3 + 4 + 6 + 12 = 28$

The sum of the factors is greater than 2×12, so **12** is an abundant number. The sum of the factors is greater than **2n**, where **n** represents the original number.

Additive Inverse

The number that, when added to another number, yields zero.

Example:
$+3 + -3 = 0$
-3 is the additive inverse of +3.

Binomial

A math expression that has two terms.

Examples:
$5 + 11$
$2x + 4$
$3x + 2y$

Coefficient

The numerical part of an algebraic term.

Examples:
$3x^2$ **3** is the coefficient.
$2y$ **2** is the coefficient.
$5(a + b)$ **5** is the coefficient.

Algebraic Ideas

Deficient Number

A number in which the sum of its factors is less than two times the number.

Example:
4 = 1, 2, 4
1 + 2 + 4 = 7

The sum of the factors is less than 2 x 4, so **4** is a deficient number. The sum of the factors is less than **2n**, where **n** represents the original number.

Equation

A number sentence that uses the equal sign. Everything on one side of an equal sign (=) has to equal everything on the other side.

Examples:
8 + 4 = 12
4 x 5 = 20
7 – 3 = 4
9 ÷ 3 = 3
35 – 23 = 10 + 2
7 + 4 + 3 = 2 x 7

Exponent

A small symbol placed above and to the right of a number or letter that shows how many times the base is to be multiplied by itself.

6^4 ← exponent

↑
base

Example:
$6^4 = 6 \times 6 \times 6 \times 6$, so $6^4 = 1,296$
$b^3 = b \times b \times b$
$5^7 = 5 \times 5 \times 5 \times 5 \times 5 \times 5 \times 5$, so $5^7 = 78,125$
$7^2 = 7 \times 7$, so $7^2 = 49$

There are several rules that can help when solving problems with exponents:

✪ First Power

Any number raised to the first power always equals the base.

Examples:
$7^1 = 7$
$23^1 = 23$

✪ Negative Numbers and Even Powers

If a negative number is raised to an even power, the answer will always be a positive.

Examples:
$-2^4 = 16$
$-5^4 = 625$

Algebraic Ideas

Exponent, continued

✪ Negative Numbers and Odd Powers

If a negative number is raised to an odd power, the answer will always be a negative.

Examples:
$-3^3 = -27$
$-2^5 = -32$

✪ Positive Numbers

If a positive number is raised to a power, the answer will always be positive.

Examples:
$2^3 = 8$
$4^2 = 16$

✪ Zero

Any number other than zero raised to the zero power will equal one.

Examples:
$7^0 = 1$
$36^0 = 1$

Exponential Numbers

Numbers that have an exponent. See *Exponent*.

Fibonacci Sequence

A sequence of numbers discovered by Leonardo Pisano, who called himself Fibonacci. In this number sequence, which is found often in nature, each number is the sum of the two numbers that came before it.

Example:
1, 1, 2, 3, 5, 8, 13, 21, . . .

Finite Set

A set that has a specific number of members.

Algebraic Ideas

Formula

A set of symbols that expresses a mathematical fact or rule. A short way of writing the rule for a specific equation.

Examples:
$a = l \times w$ (area of a square)
$p = 2l + 2w$ (perimeter of a square)
$a = \pi r^2$ (area of a circle)
$c = 2\pi r$ or πd (circumference of a circle)

Formulas, Common

There are many common formulas that can be used to solve math problems.

b = base B = area of base d = diameter h = height l = length
π = pi (3.14 . . .) r = radius s = side w = width

Area
circle: $\pi r^2 = a$
rectangle: $l \times w = a$
square: $s^2 = a$
triangle: $\frac{1}{2}bh = a$

Circumference: $c = \pi d$ or $c = 2\pi r$

Perimeter
circle: see *Circumference*, above
rectangle: $2(l + w) = p$
square: $4s = p$
triangle: $a + b + c = p$, where a, b, and c represent each side

Volume
cone: $\frac{1}{3}\pi r^2 h = v$
cube: $s^3 = v$
cylinder: $\pi r^2 h = v$
rectangular or triangular prism: $l \times w \times h = v$ or $bh = v$
pyramid: $\frac{1}{3}bh = v$
sphere: $\frac{4}{3}\pi r^3 = v$

Identity Element

A number that does not change the value of another number when a certain operation is performed.

Identity Element, continued
✪ Addition and Subtraction
0 is the identity element.

Examples:
0 + 3 = 3
7 − 0 = 7

✪ Multiplication and Division
1 is the identity element.

Examples:
1 x 5 = 5
8 ÷ 1 = 8

Inequality
Not equal. A statement in which one expression is greater than (>), less than (<), or not equal (≠) to another. The symbol for inequality is ≠.

Infinite Set
A set that has an unlimited number of members.

Multiplication of Integers
Positive and negative integers can be multiplied using the following rules:

✪ Different Sign
When two integers with different signs [(+, -) or (-, +)] are multiplied, the product is negative.

Examples:
+6 x -4 = -24
-8 x +2 = -16

✪ Same Sign
When two integers with the same sign [(+, +) or (-, -)] are multiplied, the product is positive.

Examples:
+7 x +5 = +35
-4 x -3 = +12

Multiplicative Inverse
See *Reciprocal*.

Algebraic Ideas

Negative Integer

A number less than zero. See *Negative Number*.

Negative Number

An amount, or quantity, less than zero. These numbers are written with a negative sign in front of them, such as -5, -26, or -100. On a number line, these are the numbers to the left of zero. Negative numbers are also called negative integers.

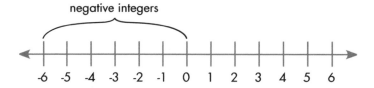

negative integers

Number Sentence

A statement that involves numbers and their relationship or equality. Number sentences can be true, false, or open.

Examples:	
5 x 9 = 45	true
9 + 11 = 4	false
6 + _ = 17	open

Origin

In a coordinate system or graph, the point where the axes intersect. The origin (base point) is (0, 0).

Pascal's Triangle

An array of numbers made popular by Blaise Pascal. One use of the triangle is finding the binomial coefficients for expressions like $(x + y)^2$. The triangle has a number pattern in which each number is the sum of the two numbers above it.

Perfect Number

A number in which the sum of its factors equals two times the number.

Example:
6 = 1, 2, 3, 6
1 + 2 + 3 + 6 = 12
The sum of its factors equals 2 x 6, so **6** is a perfect number.

Pi

The ratio between the circumference of a circle and its diameter. Pi's symbol is the 16th letter of the Greek alphabet, so it is written as π. Pi is approximately 3.14159265. . . . It is a nonterminating decimal, which means it goes on forever. Pi is very often rounded to the hundredths place, 3.14, to make it easier to use.

Example:

$$\pi = \frac{\text{circumference}}{\text{diameter}} \quad \pi = \frac{c}{d} \quad d \times 3.14 = c$$

Positive Integer

A number greater than zero. See *Positive Number*.

Positive Number

An amount, or quantity, greater than zero. On a number line, these numbers are to the right of zero. Positive numbers are also called *positive integers*.

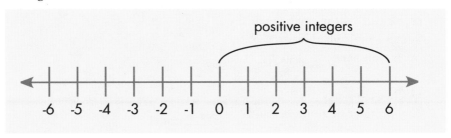

Algebraic Ideas

Power

The result of the repeated multiplication of a number by itself. These problems are read as "to the *n*th power," and they are generally written using an exponent.

Examples:
6^4 is read as "6 to the 4th power."
$6^4 = 6 \times 6 \times 6 \times 6 = 1,296$ 1,296 is the fourth power of 6.
$3^2 = 3 \times 3 = 9$ 9 is the second power of 3.
$2^5 = 2 \times 2 \times 2 \times 2 \times 2 = 32$ 32 is the fifth power of 2.

Properties

✪ Associative (Grouping) Property

Changing the grouping of the numbers does not change the sum or product.

Examples:
$(2 \times 3) \times 4 = 24$ $2 \times (3 \times 4) = 24$
$6 \times 4 = 24$ $2 \times 12 = 24$

✪ Commutative (Order) Property

Changing the order of the addends or factors does not change the sum or product.

Examples:
$7 + 3 = 10$ $6 \times 5 = 30$
$3 + 7 = 10$ $5 \times 6 = 30$

✪ Distributive Property

The product of a number and the sum of two numbers is the same as the sum of the products of the number multiplied by each of the other numbers.

Example:
$3 (4 + 5) = (3 \times 4) + (3 \times 5)$
$3 \times 9 = 12 + 15$
$27 = 27$

✪ One Property

The product of a number and 1 is that number, while the quotient of a number divided by 1 is that number.

Examples:
$7 \times 1 = 7$ $329 \div 1 = 329$

Properties, continued

✪ Zero Property

When adding zero to or subtracting zero from a number, the answer is that number. When multiplying a number by zero, the answer is zero.

Examples:
$6 + 0 = 6$
$113 - 0 = 113$
$248 \times 0 = 0$

Real Numbers

The set of rational and irrational numbers. Any number that is positive, negative, or zero.

Significant Digit

A digit that affects the value of a number.

Examples:

0.73   The zero does not affect the value of this number, so it is not significant.

5.08   The zero holds the tenths place open in this number, and it affects the value of the number. Therefore, it is significant.

Square

To multiply a number by itself or raise a number to the second power.

Example:
$9^2 = 9 \times 9 = 81$

Square Root

The number that, when squared (multiplied by itself), will produce a given number. The symbol for square root is $\sqrt{\ }$.

Examples: 3 is the square root of 9   4 is the square root of 16

Algebraic Ideas

47

Subset

A set that is part of another set. The symbol for a subset is ⊂.

Example:
{1, 3, 5, 7} is a subset of {1, 2, 3, 4, 5, 6, 7, 8}
{1, 3, 5, 7} ⊂ {1, 2, 3, 4, 5, 6, 7, 8}

Symbol

A letter or mark that stands for a quantity, operation, or relationship.

Common Symbols

+	addition	=	equal	¢	penny, cent
...	and so on	!	factorial	%	percent
∠	angle	'	feet	⊥	perpendicular
≈	approximately equal to	≥	greater than or equal to	π	3.14 . . .
∴∴	averaged with	"	inch	±	plus or minus
⊙	circle	∞	infinity	^	to the power of . . .
≅	congruent to	≠	inequality	→	ray
↔	corresponds to	∩	intersection	≈	similar to
.	decimal	≤	less than or equal to	√	square root
°	degree	—	line segment	⊂	is a subset of
÷	division	×	multiplication	–	subtraction
/	division, fraction	•	multiplication	|	such that . . .
$	dollar	-	negative number	∴	therefore . . .
∈	element of	∉	not an element of	△	triangle
∅	empty set	‖	parallel	∪	union

Unknown

The symbol in an equation for which a solution must be found that will make the equation true.

Example:
$3y - 5 = 10$ y is the unknown.

Variable

A quantity that can have several different values. Anything that changes.

Geometry

Adjacent

To lie or stand near. Adjacent figures are near or beside each other without being separated by other figures.

Adjacent Angles

Two angles that have a common vertex and one common side.

Example:
∠BAK and ∠KAD are adjacent angles.

Adjoining

Sharing a common boundary.

Alternate Exterior Angles

Exterior angles formed by a set of parallel lines intersected by a third line. These angles have the same measure of degrees and are the same size.

Examples:
∠M and ∠D are alternate exterior angles.
∠A and ∠N are alternate exterior angles.

Alternate Interior Angles

Interior angles formed by a set of parallel lines intersected by a third line. These angles have the same measure of degrees and are the same size.

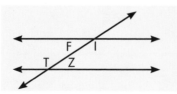

Examples:
∠T and ∠I are alternate interior angles.
∠F and ∠Z are alternate interior angles.

Geometry

Altitude

See *Height*.

Angle

The figure made by two straight lines meeting at a point (a vertex) or by two rays meeting at a point. The difference between the two lines is measured in degrees.

360° = a whole circle
180° = a half (semi) circle
90° = a quarter circle

✪ **Acute Angle**

An angle smaller than 90 degrees.

✪ **Obtuse Angle**

An angle larger than 90 degrees but less than 180 degrees.

✪ **Right Angle**

An angle that has the same shape as the corner of a square. A right angle equals 90 degrees.

✪ **Straight Angle**

An angle that measures 180 degrees.

Arc

A part of the circumference of a circle. A part of the edge between any two points on a circle.

Geometry

Arc, continued

✪ **Major Arc**

An arc that is greater than or equal to 180°.

✪ **Minor Arc**

An arc that is less than or equal to 180°.

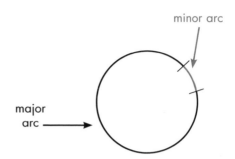

Axis

One of the perpendicular lines used to form a graph. The x-axis (abscissa) is the horizontal axis, and the y-axis (ordinate) is the vertical axis.

Base

The line segment that is the foundation of a geometric figure.

Bisect

To divide into two equal parts.

Bisector

The straight line or ray that bisects (divides) a line or angle into two congruent portions.

Center

A point equally distant from all points on the circumference of a circle or surface of a sphere.

Center Point

See *Center*.

Math Dictionary for Kids

Central Angle

An angle whose end points are
on the circumference of a circle
and whose vertex is at the circle's
center point.

central
angle →

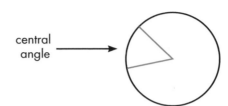

Chord

A line that connects two points
on a circle. A diameter is a
special kind of chord that passes
through the center of the circle.

Circle

A closed curve in which all of
the points are the same distance
from the point in the center. The
distance from the center of the
circle to any point on the circle is
the radius.

radius

Circumference

The outer boundary, or perimeter, of a circle or circular surface. The
distance around the outside of a circle or circular object.

Formula:
C = 3.14 x diameter   (C = π • d)
   or
C = 2 x 3.14 x radius   (C = 2 • π • r)

Closed Figure

A two-dimensional figure that does not have an opening to the outside.
All of the figure's lines or curves meet to close the shape.

Geometry

Collinear

Lying on the same straight line.

     Points A, B, and C are collinear.

Compass

A tool used for drawing circles.

Complementary Angles

Two angles whose sum equals 90°.

Example:
∠ABC and ∠CBD are complementary angles.

Concentric

Sharing a common center.

Cone

A solid figure that has a circular bottom and one flat face.

Congruent

Figures that have the same size and shape. The symbol for congruency is ≅.

       △ABC ≅ △DEF

Coordinates

The two numbers in a number pair used to find or define the position of a point or line. Also called a number pair and an ordered pair. The first number in the pair refers to the location on the x-axis, while the second number refers to the location on the y-axis.

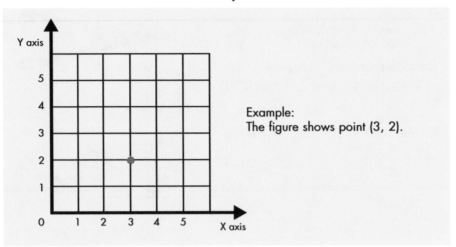

Example:
The figure shows point (3, 2).

Coplanar Lines

Two parallel or intersecting lines that rest in the same plane.

Corresponding Angles

Pairs of equal angles that are created when parallel lines are intersected by a third line. Four sets of corresponding angles are formed at the intersection. Corresponding angles are the same size in degrees.

Example:
∠X and ∠N are corresponding angles.
∠Q and ∠P are corresponding angles.

Corresponding Parts

Parts, such as points, sides, or angles, of two congruent figures that have the same position and are the same size.

Corresponding Parts, continued

Example:
Side AC corresponds to DF and ∠A
corresponds to ∠D.

Cube

A three-dimensional figure that
has 6 square faces, 8 vertices, and
12 edges.

Cylinder

A three-dimensional figure that
has two circles for faces.

Decagon

A polygon with 10 sides and 10 angles. Also called a 10-gon.

Deltoid

See *Kite*.

Diagonal

A line extending in a slanting manner across opposite corners in a
polygon.

Diameter

A special kind of chord that passes through the center of a circle joining two opposite points. The length of a diameter is equal to two radii. The diameter divides a circle into two equal parts called semicircles.

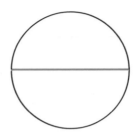

Dimension

The number of basic units used to measure a geometric figure.

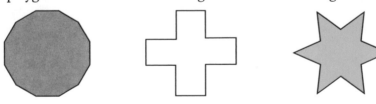

- one-dimensional ———
- two-dimensional ▢
- three-dimensional ◼

Dodecagon

A polygon with 12 sides and 12 angles. Also called a 12-gon.

Edge

A straight line segment that is the intersection of two faces of a solid figure. The place where faces come together or meet.

Edge
Edge
Edge

Ellipse

An oval. A closed plane curve that has two centers (foci) that define the shape and size of the outer perimeter.

End Point

The point that marks the end of a line segment or ray.

end points

Equiangular

Having all angles equal. A square is equiangular.

Equilateral

Having all sides equal.

Exterior

Outside a figure.

Exterior Angle

An angle on the outside of a polygon that is formed by the extension of one side and the adjacent side of the polygon.

Face

One of the plane figures that make up a space figure.

Face

Face

Face

Geometry

Flip

To turn over.

Front View

The view of something from the front.

Height

The vertical distance from the base to the highest point. Also called *altitude*.

In a triangle, the height is the perpendicular distance from the vertex to the opposite side.

Hemisphere

Half a sphere.

Heptagon

A polygon with seven sides and seven angles. Also called a 7-gon.

Hexagon

A polygon with six sides and six angles. Also called a 6-gon.

Horizontal

Parallel to the horizon and perpendicular to vertical.

Horizontal Symmetry

See *Line Symmetry*.

Hypotenuse

The side of a right triangle that is opposite of the right angle.

Icosagon

A polygon with 20 sides and 20 angles. Also called a 20-gon.

Image

The visual picture, or likeness, of something produced by the reflection from a mirror.

Geometry

Inscribed Angle

An angle in which all of its points lie on the circle's circumference.

Interior

Inside a figure.

Interior Angle

An angle on the inside of a polygon that is formed by two adjacent sides of the polygon.

Intersecting Lines

Lines that meet at a point.

Irregular Polygon

A polygon in which not all of the sides are the same length, and not all angles have the same measure. See *Polygon*.

Kite

A quadrilateral with two pairs of equal sides; each pair shares a vertex. In a kite, the angles of unequal sides are equal, and the diagonals intersect at right angles. Also called a deltoid.

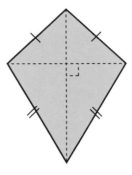

Line

A one-dimensional straight path that is endless in both directions.

Line Segment

A portion (part) of a straight line. There is a point at each end of a line segment, and sometimes the ends will be labeled.

Line Symmetry

✪ Horizontal Symmetry
Parallel to the horizon.

✪ Vertical Symmetry
Perpendicular to the horizon.

Midpoint

A point that is equal distance from the two endpoints of a line segment.

midpoint

Net

A diagram that shows the edges of an unfolded polyhedron (a three-dimensional figure). There can be more than one net for each polyhedron.

Cube   Tetrahedron (pyramid)

Geometry

Nonagon

A polygon with nine sides and nine angles. Also called a 9-gon.

Noncollinear Points

Three points that do not lie in the same straight line.

Number Pair

A pair of numbers that is used to give the location of a point on a graph. Also called coordinates.

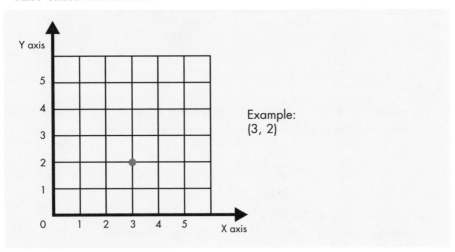

Example:
(3, 2)

Octagon

A polygon with eight sides and eight angles. Also called an 8-gon.

Open Figure

A two-dimensional figure that is not closed all the way. It has a place where its lines or curves do not meet.

Origin

In a coordinate system or graph, the point where the axes intersect. The origin (base point) is (0, 0).

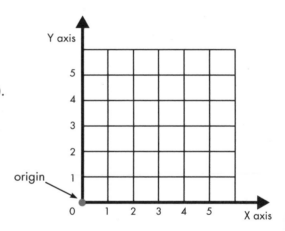

Parallel Lines

Lines that do not intersect (cross) and would not ever cross if they were extended. Lines that are equidistant at all points.

Parallelogram

A quadrilateral that has two pairs of opposite sides that are both equal and parallel. In a parallelogram, opposite angles are equal (congruent), and adjacent angles are supplementary.

Pentagon

A polygon with five sides and five angles. Also called a 5-gon.

Perimeter

The distance around the outside of a figure. The sum of the length of the sides of a geometric figure.

Example:
perimeter = a + b + c + d

Perpendicular Lines

Lines that intersect to form a right (90°) angle. Lines that form a square corner.

Pi

The ratio between the circumference of a circle and its diameter. Pi's symbol is the 16th letter of the Greek alphabet, so it is written as π. Pi is approximately 3.14159265. . . . It is a nonterminating decimal, which means it goes on forever. Pi is very often rounded to the hundredths place, 3.14, to make it easier to use.

Example:

$$\pi = \frac{\text{circumference}}{\text{diameter}} \qquad \pi = \frac{c}{d} \qquad d \times 3.14 = c$$

Geometry

Plane Figure

A flat shape having two dimensions, length and width, and all points located within the same plane.

Polygon

A closed figure that is formed entirely by line segments. Examples include pentagons, hexagons, heptagons, octagons, trapezoids, and squares.

✪ Irregular Polygon

Not all of the sides of a figure are the same length, and not all of the angles have the same measure.

✪ Regular Polygon

All of the sides of the figure are the same length, and all of the angles have the same measure.

Polyhedron

A three-dimensional figure with many faces, such as a cube, pyramid, and prism.

Prism

A solid figure whose ends are parallel, congruent (equal in size and shape) polygons, and whose sides are parallelograms.

Geometry

Protractor

An instrument in the shape of a semicircle used for drawing and measuring angles in degrees.

Pyramid

A geometric solid formed by triangles. The faces on a pyramid are triangles that meet at a point (vertex). They can have different shaped bases and are named by the shape of their base.

triangular pyramid   square pyramid   rectangular pyramid

Pythagorean Theorem

A theorem that the sum of the squares of the two sides of a right triangle is equal to the square of the hypotenuse.

Example:
$a^2 + b^2 = c^2$
$4^2 + 3^2 = 5^2$
$16 + 9 = 25$

Geometry

Quadrant

A quarter of a plane figure that has been divided by perpendicular lines. Circles can be divided into quadrants. In coordinate geometry, the plane is divided into four quadrants by the x-axis and the y-axis.

 1 quadrant

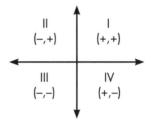

Quadrilateral

Any polygon with four sides.

Examples:
square   rectangle
parallelogram   rhomboid
rhombus   trapezoid
trapezium

Radius

A straight line that extends from the center of a circle to a point on the circumference of a circle. The radius equals one half of the diameter.

Ray

A straight line that extends from a point forever in one direction.

Rectangle

A quadrilateral and parallelogram that has four right angles and two pairs of opposite sides that are the same length.

Geometry

Rectangular Prism

A space figure that has rectangles and squares for faces. Rectangular prisms are in the shape of a box, and they have 6 faces, 8 vertices, and 12 edges.

Reflection

The image of an object as seen in a mirror. Reflection is useful in finding symmetry.

Regular Polygon

A polygon in which all of the sides and all of the angles are congruent. If a circle is drawn around a regular polygon, all of its vertices will touch the circumference. See *Polygon*.

Geometry

Rhomboid

A quadrilateral and parallelogram in which opposite sides are parallel, but there are no right angles. Adjacent sides are not equal.

Rhombus

A quadrilateral and parallelogram that has four equal sides.

Rotate

To turn or move an object around a point.

Rotation

To turn around a center point.

Rotational Symmetry

A figure is said to have rotational symmetry if it can be turned, or rotated, to fit on itself and still look the same. If it only fits on itself one time (a turn of 360°), it does not have rotational symmetry. Rotational symmetry is named for the number of ways a shape can turn to fit on itself. For example, if it can be turned onto itself exactly three times, it is said to have an Order 3 rotational symmetry.

Segment

Any of the parts into which something can be separated. A piece or portion of something, such as a line.

Semicircle

A half circle.

Side View

The view of something from the side.

Similar Figures

Figures that have the same shape, but not the same size.

Slide

To move an object or figure without flipping or rotating it.

Slope

The amount of slant or inclination of a line on a coordinate graph.

Example:

$$\text{slope} = \frac{\text{change in } y}{\text{change in } x}$$

Geometry

Space Figure

Another way to describe a three-dimensional shape. Space figures have volume, meaning they take up space.

Sphere

A space figure shaped like a round ball in which every point is equidistant (the same distance) from the center.

Square

A quadrilateral and parallelogram that has four equal sides and four equal 90° angles (right angles). A square is a special type of rectangle.

Supplementary Angles

Two angles whose sum equals 180°.

Example:
∠ABC + ∠CBD = 180°

Surface Area

The sum of the areas of all of the flat surfaces on a three-dimensional figure.

Symmetrical

A figure can be considered symmetrical if it has line symmetry, rotational symmetry, or both. Line symmetry is characteristic of a figure that can be folded into two identical halves, or reflected or flipped over a line, yet appears unchanged. Rotational symmetry is the number of ways a shape can be turned, or rotated, to fit on itself and still look the same. If it only fits on itself one time (a turn of 360°), it does not have rotational symmetry. See *Line Symmetry and Rotational Symmetry*.

Geometry

Tangent

A line that touches a figure at one point, but does not intersect it.

Top View

The view of something from the top.

Transversal

A straight line that intersects, or crosses, a set of lines.

transversal

Trapezium

A quadrilateral in which no two sides are parallel.

Trapezoid

A quadrilateral that has exactly one pair of parallel sides.

Triangle

A plane figure with three segments as sides and three angles. The sum of a triangle's angles equals 180 degrees.

Geometry

Triangle, continued

✪ Equilateral Triangle
A triangle in which all three sides
are the same length and all three
angles are 60°.

✪ Isosceles Triangle
A triangle that has two sides of
the same length.

✪ Right Triangle
A triangle that has a right (90°)
angle.

✪ Scalene Triangle
A triangle in which no sides are
the same length.

Triangular Prism
A solid figure that has two
triangular and three rectangular
faces, six vertices, and nine edges.

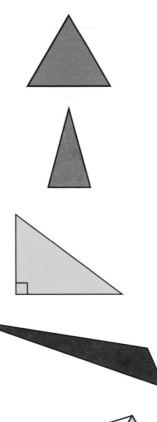

Turn
See *Rotate*.

Geometry

Vertex

The point of intersection of rays or line segments. The place where lines or edges meet, or corners. In plane figures, the point opposite the base.

  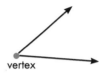

Vertical

Perpendicular to the horizon, or upright.

Vertical Symmetry

See *Line Symmetry*.

Vertically Opposite Angles

Sets of angles that form when two lines intersect. Angles with a common vertex whose sides are extensions of the other angle's sides. Vertical angles lie on opposite sides of the same vertex and are the same size.

Example:
∠A and ∠C are vertically opposite.
∠B and ∠D are vertically opposite.

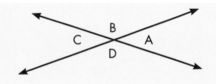

Vertices

The plural of vertex. More than one vertex. See Vertex.

Geometry

Decimals, Fractions, Percents, and Ratios

Adding Decimals

1. Line up the decimal points so that the place value is in line.
2. Add as normal. Zeros can be added after the decimal point in order to make adding easier, and it won't change the answer.
3. Bring the decimal point straight down into the answer.

Examples:

$$.75 + 2 + 1.674 =$$

$$\begin{array}{r} .750 \\ 2.000 \\ + \ 1.674 \\ \hline 4.424 \end{array}$$

$$3.5 + .46 =$$

$$\begin{array}{r} 3.50 \\ + \ .46 \\ \hline 3.96 \end{array}$$

$$.4 + 3 + .27 =$$

$$\begin{array}{r} .40 \\ 3.00 \\ + \ .27 \\ \hline 3.67 \end{array}$$

Adding Fractions

To add fractions, first look at the denominators.

✪ Same Denominators

1. Leave the denominator the same, and write it in your answer.
2. Add the numerators.
3. Write the sum over the denominator.
4. Reduce (simplify) if needed.

Examples:

$$\frac{7}{12} + \frac{4}{12} = \frac{11}{12}$$

$$\frac{3}{7} + \frac{2}{7} = \frac{5}{7}$$

$$\frac{4}{8} + \frac{2}{8} = \frac{6}{8} \div \frac{2}{2} = \frac{3}{4}$$

✪ Different Denominators

1. Find a common denominator.
2. Make equivalent fractions.
3. Add the numerators.
4. Write the sum over the common denominator.
5. Reduce (simplify) if needed.

Adding Fractions, continued
○ Different Denominators, continued

Examples:

$$\frac{2}{7} + \frac{3}{21} =$$

$$\frac{2}{7} \times \frac{3}{3} = \frac{6}{21}$$
$$+\frac{3}{21} \quad = \frac{3}{21}$$
$$\frac{9}{21}{\tiny\frac{\div 3}{\div 3}} = \frac{3}{7}$$

$$\frac{1}{2} + \frac{1}{3} =$$

$$\frac{1}{2} \times \frac{3}{3} = \frac{3}{6}$$
$$+\frac{1}{3} \times \frac{2}{2} = \frac{2}{6}$$
$$\frac{5}{6}$$

Changing a Decimal to a Fraction
See *Converting Decimals.*

Changing a Decimal to a Percent
See *Converting Decimals.*

Changing a Percent to a Decimal
See *Converting Percents.*

Changing Improper Fractions to Mixed or Whole Numbers
See *Converting Fractions.*

Changing Mixed Numbers to Improper Fractions
See *Converting Fractions.*

Common Denominator
See *Denominator.*

Comparing Decimals
To determine which decimal is larger or smaller, place value must be compared.

1. Line up the decimal points.
2. Compare tenths, then hundredths, and then thousandths.

.7____.08   means the same as   .70____.08

7 tenths is larger than 0 tenths

Comparing Decimals, continued

1. Line up decimal points   0.41
                                       0.275

2. Look at place value: 4 tenths is larger than 2 tenths, so **0.41** is larger than **0.275**

Comparing Fractions

There are several ways to compare fractions.

✪ Method 1: Convert Fractions to Decimals

Write each fraction as a division problem, divide to find the decimals, and then compare the decimal numbers to determine which is larger.

Example:

$$\frac{5}{7} \underline{} \frac{2}{3}$$

$$7\overline{)4\,\overset{5}{5}.\,{}^{1}00}\qquad 3\overline{)\overset{1}{2}.\,{}^{1}00}$$

$$
\begin{array}{r} .71 \\ -4\,9 \\ \hline 10 \\ -7 \\ \hline 3 \end{array}
\qquad
\begin{array}{r} .66 \\ -1\ 8 \\ \hline 20 \\ -18 \\ \hline 2 \end{array}
$$

.71 is greater than .66, so $\frac{5}{7}$ is greater than $\frac{2}{3}$.

✪ Method 2: Cross Multiply

Multiply the numerator of one fraction by the denominator of the other. Repeat the process with the other two numbers, and compare the two products to determine which fraction is larger.

Example:

$$\frac{8}{12} \diagdown\!\!\!\!\diagup \frac{4}{7}$$

7 x 8 = 56
12 x 4 = 48
56 is greater than 48, so 8/12 is greater than 4/7.

✪ Method 3: Find a Common Denominator

Find a common denominator for both fractions, and then compare the two fractions to determine which is larger.

Decimals, Fractions, Percents, and Ratios

Comparing Fractions, continued
✪ Method 3: Find a Common Denominator, continued

To find a common denominator, multiply or divide both the numerator and denominator of a fraction or fractions by the same number. Sometimes you will only need to adjust one of the fractions.

$$\frac{1}{2} \times \frac{5}{5} = \frac{5}{10} \qquad \frac{2}{3} \times \frac{2}{2} = \frac{4}{6}$$

$$\frac{3}{5} \times \frac{2}{2} = \frac{6}{10} \qquad \frac{3}{6}$$

Now that they have a common denominator, they can be compared, added, or subtracted easily.

Complex Fraction

A complex fraction has a mixed or fractional number for its numerator or denominator.

Example:

$$\frac{\frac{1}{2}}{\frac{3}{4}}$$

Converting Decimals

✪ Decimal to Fraction
To change a decimal to a fraction, use place value.

1. Decide whether the decimal represents tenths, hundredths, thousandths, etc.
2. Write the numerical part of the decimal over the appropriate power of 10— over 10 if the decimal was in the tenths place, over 100 if the decimal was in the hundredths place, and so on.
3. Reduce the fraction.

Example:
.05 is 5 hundredths $\frac{5}{100}$ $\frac{5}{100} \div \frac{5}{5} = \frac{1}{20}$

✪ Decimal to Percent
To change a decimal to a percent, move the decimal point.

1. Move the decimal point two places to the right.
2. Add a percent sign (%).
3. Add zeros for placeholders if necessary.

Converting Decimals, continued
✪ Decimal to Percent, continued

Examples:

.56 = 56%   .489 = 48.9%

.05 = 5%   .3 = 30%

Converting Fractions
✪ Fraction to Decimal

To find the decimal for a fraction: ⅝

1. Divide the numerator by the denominator

$$8\overline{)5}$$

2. Add a decimal point and 0's to the dividend. Bring the decimal point straight up to the quotient.

$$8\overline{)5.00}$$

3. Divide as normal; write the answer with the decimal point.

$$
\begin{array}{r}
.625 \\
8\overline{)5.00} \\
-48 \\
\hline
20 \\
-16 \\
\hline
40 \\
-40 \\
\hline
0
\end{array}
$$

✪ Improper Fraction to Mixed or Whole Number

To convert an improper fraction to a mixed or whole number, use division.

1. Divide the numerator by the denominator.
2. Write the remainder as a fraction.

$$\frac{26}{4} \rightarrow 4\overline{)26} \rightarrow 4\overline{)\begin{array}{r}6 \\ 26 \\ -24 \\ \hline 2\end{array}} \rightarrow 6\frac{2}{4} \rightarrow 6\frac{1}{2}$$

Converting Fractions, continued

✪ Mixed Number to Improper Fraction

To convert a mixed number to an improper fraction, use multiplication.

1. Multiply the denominator by the whole number.
2. Add the numerator to the answer.
3. Put the answer over the original denominator.

$$5\frac{3}{7} = 5\frac{^{+}3}{^{\times}7} = \frac{38}{7} \quad \text{or} \quad 5\frac{3}{7} = \frac{(5\times7)+3}{7} = \frac{38}{7}$$

$7 \times 5 = 35$
$35 + 3 = 38$
$^{38}/_{7}$

$7 \times 5 + 3$
The denominator stays the same.

Converting Percents

✪ Percent to a Decimal

To change a percentage to a decimal, move the decimal point two places to the left. Add zeros as placeholders if necessary.

Examples:
56% = .56
5% = .05

48.9% = .489

Decimal

A special kind of fraction that has a power of 10 (10, 100, 1,000, 10,000, . . .) for a denominator. Decimals are part of a whole. They are written with a decimal point, using place value, instead of as a fraction.

AND ● _____
tenths
hundredths
thousandths
ten thousandth

Decimal Fraction

A fraction whose denominator is a power of 10, such as 10, 100, or 1,000.

Examples:
$\frac{2}{10} = .2$ $\frac{34}{100} = .34$ $\frac{56}{1000} = .056$

Decimal Point

A dot written in a number that separates the whole number from the fractional part. The decimal point is read as "and."

Denominator

The number that is written below the line in a fraction. It shows into how many equal pieces the whole has been divided.

Example

$$\frac{6}{8}$$ 8 is the denominator

✪ Common Denominator

A common multiple of the denominators of two or more fractions.

Example:

$^1/_2$ Multiples of 2:   2   4   6   8   **10**   12   14   16   18   **20**   22 . . .
$^3/_5$ Multiples of 5:   5   **10**   15   **20**   25   30   35   40   45   50   55 . . .

10 and 20 are multiples of 2 and 5, so **10** and **20** are common denominators of $^1/_2$ and $^3/_5$.

Using 10 as a common denominator, multiply both the numerator and denominator of one fraction by the number needed to produce a denominator of 10. Repeat for the second fraction. The numbers by which the fractions are multiplied will usually be different for each fraction.

$$\frac{1}{2} \times \frac{5}{5} = \frac{5}{10}$$

Now that the fractions have a common denominator, they can be compared, added, or subtracted easily.

$$\frac{3}{5} \times \frac{2}{2} = \frac{6}{10}$$

$$\frac{2}{3} \times \frac{2}{2} = \frac{4}{6}$$

$$\frac{3}{6}$$

Sometimes you will only need to adjust one of the fractions. The fractions now can be compared, added, or subtracted.

Decimals, Fractions, Percents, and Ratios

Denominator, continued

✪ Lowest Common Denominator (LCD)

The lowest denominator that two or more fractions have in common.

Example:
$\frac{1}{2}$ Multiples of 2: 2 4 **6** 8 10 12 14 16 . . .
$\frac{2}{3}$ Multiples of 3: 3 **6** 9 12 15 18 21 24 . . .

6 is the lowest common multiple of 2 and 3, so it is the lowest common denominator (LCD) of $\frac{1}{2}$ and $\frac{2}{3}$.

$$\frac{1}{2} = \frac{3}{6} \quad and \quad \frac{2}{3} = \frac{4}{6}$$

Dividing Decimals

1. Write the problem as normal.
2. Bring the decimal point straight up.
3. Divide as normal.

$$6 \overline{)\, 4.26} \quad \begin{array}{r} 0.71 \\ \hline \end{array} = 0.71$$

$$\begin{array}{r} 0.71 \\ 6\overline{)\,4.26} \\ -42 \\ \hline 06 \\ -\ 6 \\ \hline 0 \end{array} = 0.71$$

Dividing Fractions

When fractions are divided, a reciprocal and multiplication must be used. To find a fraction's reciprocal, invert the fraction by writing the numerator on the bottom and the denominator on the top. After the fraction has been inverted, multiply the two fractions together.

✪ To divide regular fractions:

1. Invert the divisor to find the reciprocal.
2. Multiply the numerators.
3. Multiply the denominators.
4. Change the answer to a mixed or whole number.
5. Reduce (simplify) the answer if necessary.

$$\frac{4}{7} \div \frac{2}{3} = \frac{4}{7} \cdot \frac{3}{2} = \frac{12}{14} \div \frac{2}{2} = \frac{6}{7}$$

✪ To divide improper fractions:

1. Invert the divisor.
2. Multiply the numerators.
3. Multiply the denominators.

Dividing Fractions, continued

✪ To divide improper fractions, continued

4. Change the answer to a mixed or whole number.
5. Reduce (simplify) the answer if necessary.

$$\frac{7}{3} \div \frac{8}{4} = \frac{7}{3} \cdot \frac{4}{8} = \frac{28}{24} = 1\frac{4}{24} \div \frac{4}{4} = 1\frac{1}{6}$$

✪ To divide fractions with mixed numbers:

1. Change any mixed numbers to improper fractions.
2. Invert the divisor.
3. Multiply the numerators.
4. Multiply the denominators.
5. Change the answer to a mixed or whole number.
6. Reduce (simplify) the answer if necessary.

$$1\frac{2}{3} \div 2\frac{1}{4} = \frac{5}{3} \div \frac{9}{4} = \frac{5}{3} \cdot \frac{4}{9} = \frac{20}{27}$$

$$3\frac{5}{7} \div 4\frac{2}{3} = \frac{26}{7} \div \frac{14}{3} = \frac{26}{7} \cdot \frac{3}{14} = \frac{78}{98} \div \frac{2}{2} = \frac{39}{49}$$

✪ To divide fractions and whole numbers:

1. Change any whole number to its fractional equivalent.
2. Invert the divisor.
3. Multiply the numerators.
4. Multiply the denominators.
5. Change the answer to a mixed or whole number.
6. Reduce (simplify) the answer if necessary.

$$3 \div \frac{4}{5} = \frac{3}{1} \div \frac{4}{5} = \frac{3}{1} \cdot \frac{5}{4} = \frac{15}{4} = 3\frac{3}{4}$$

$$1\frac{3}{4} \div 6 = \frac{7}{4} \div \frac{6}{1} = \frac{7}{4} \cdot \frac{1}{6} = \frac{7}{24}$$

Eighth

One of eight equal parts.

$3/8$ is shown.

Eleventh
One of 11 equal parts.

$^{10}/_{11}$ is shown.

Equivalent Decimals
Decimals that have the same value or name the same amount.

Example:
It helps to think of money: 30 pennies (.30) equals the same amount as 3 dimes (.3).

$$0.30 = 0.3$$

 =

Equivalent Fractions
Fractions that have the same value or name the same amount of a whole.

½

²⁄₄

³⁄₆

⁴⁄₈

There are several methods to find equivalent fractions.

✪ **Method 1: Multiply or Divide**
Multiply or divide both the numerator and the denominator by the same number.

$$\frac{3}{5} \times \frac{2}{2} = \frac{6}{10} \qquad \frac{4}{7} \times \frac{3}{3} = \frac{12}{21}$$

$$\frac{16}{24} \div \frac{4}{4} = \frac{4}{6} \qquad \frac{9}{18} \div \frac{9}{9} = \frac{1}{2}$$

Equivalent Fractions, continued

✪ Method 2: Use Multiples

List the multiples for the numbers in the numerator and denominator in two separate rows. The numbers in the top row become the numerators in the equivalent fractions, while the numbers in the bottom rows become the denominators.

Example:
$$\frac{5}{8} = \begin{array}{ccccccccc} 5 & 10 & 15 & 20 & 25 & 30 & 35 & 40 & 45 \\ 8 & 16 & 24 & 32 & 40 & 48 & 56 & 64 & 72 \end{array}$$

Fifth

One of five equal parts.

 ¹/₅ is shown.

Finding a Decimal for a Fraction

See *Converting Fractions*.

Finding a Fraction of a Number

There are two methods for finding a fraction (part) of a number.

✪ Method 1: Draw It Out

Example:
³⁄₅ of 20 = 12   Break 20 into 5 groups, then look at 3 of them.

✪ Method 2: Use Division and Multiplication

1. Divide the whole number by the fraction's denominator.
2. Multiply the answer by the numerator.

Examples: ³⁄₇ of 35
1. Divide the whole number by the denominator to find one fractional part.
   35 ÷ 7 = 5
2. Multiply the answer by the numerator of the fraction. This finds the number of fractional parts.
3. ³⁄₇ of 35 = 15   15 is ³⁄₇ of 35.

Finding a Fraction of a Number, continued
✪ Method 2: Use Division and Multiplication, continued

⅔ of 27
- 27 ÷ 9 = 3
- 3 × 2 = 6
- 6 is ⅔ of 27

$\frac{4}{8}$ of 48   8)48   6 × 4 = 24

Fourth

One of four equal parts. As a fraction, it is written in simplest terms as ¼. As a decimal, ¼ is shown as .25.

¼ is shown.

Fraction

A number that shows parts of a whole or of a set. The denominator (the number below the line) tells into how many parts the whole has been divided. The numerator (the number above the line) indicates the number of those equal parts being considered.

Example:

$\frac{3}{4}$ numerator (number of parts you have)
denominator (number of parts into which the whole has been divided)

Half

One of two equal parts. As a fraction, it is written in simplest terms as ½. As a decimal, ½ is shown as .50; however, on a calculator it will be seen as .5 without an ending zero.

½ is shown.

Higher Term Fraction

A fraction whose numerator and denominator have a common factor greater than 1.

$\dfrac{2}{4}$ Factors of 2: 1, 2

     Factors of 4: 1, 2, 4

2 is a common factor of 2 and 4.

$\dfrac{2}{4}$ is in higher terms and can be reduced because 2 and 4 can both be divided by 2.

$$\dfrac{2}{4} \div \dfrac{2}{2} = \dfrac{1}{2} \qquad \dfrac{4}{12} \div \dfrac{3}{3} = \dfrac{1}{3}$$

Improper Fraction

A fraction in which the numerator is greater than the denominator and represents a value greater than 1. See also *Converting Fractions*.

Lowest Common Denominator (LCD)

See *Denominator*.

Lowest Term Fraction

A fraction whose numerator and denominator have no common factor besides 1. See *Reducing Fractions*.

Examples:

$\frac{1}{3}$ $\frac{2}{5}$

$\frac{3}{7}$ $\frac{11}{24}$

Mixed Number

A number that has both a whole number part and a fractional part, such as $2\,\frac{1}{3}$. Mixed numbers represent values greater than 1. See also *Converting Fractions*.

$3\frac{2}{3} = \frac{11}{3}$

mixed number   improper fraction

Multiplying Decimals

1. Write and solve the problem as normal.
2. Count the total number of places after each decimal in the numbers being multiplied.
3. Position the decimal the same number of places in the answer.

Multiplying Decimals, continued

$$7.56 \longrightarrow .56 \quad \text{2 places to the right of the decimal}$$
$$\times 1.2 \longrightarrow .2 \quad \text{1 place to the right of the decimal}$$
$$\underline{1512} \qquad\qquad \text{over 3 places to the left in the answer}$$
$$\underline{+7560}$$
$$9.072$$

Multiplying Fractions

The steps taken to multiply fractions depends on the type of fraction in the problem.

✪ To multiply regular fractions:

1. Multiply the numerators.
2. Multiply the denominators.
3. Reduce (simplify) the answer if necessary.

$$\frac{2}{3} \cdot \frac{4}{5} = \frac{8}{15} \qquad \frac{5}{6} \cdot \frac{2}{3} = \frac{10}{18} \div \frac{2}{2} = \frac{5}{9}$$

✪ To multiply improper fractions:

1. Multiply the numerators.
2. Multiply the denominators.
3. Change the answer to a mixed or whole number.
4. Reduce (simplify) the answer if necessary.

$$\frac{4}{3} \cdot \frac{7}{2} = \frac{28}{6} = 4\frac{4}{6} \div \frac{2}{2} = 4\frac{2}{3}$$

✪ To multiply fractions with mixed numbers:

1. Change any mixed numbers to improper fractions.
2. Multiply the numerators.
3. Multiply the denominators.
4. Change the answer to a mixed or whole number.
5. Reduce (simplify) the answer if necessary.

$$3\frac{1}{2} \cdot 2\frac{1}{3} = \frac{7}{2} \cdot \frac{7}{3} = \frac{49}{6} = 8\frac{1}{6}$$

$$1\frac{3}{4} \cdot 1\frac{1}{5} = \frac{7}{4} \cdot \frac{6}{5} = \frac{42}{20} = 2\frac{2}{20} \div \frac{2}{2} = 2\frac{1}{10}$$

Multiplying Fractions, continued

✪ To multiply fractions with whole numbers:

1. Change any whole number to its fractional equivalent.
2. Multiply the numerators.
3. Multiply the denominators.
4. Change the answer to a mixed or whole number.
5. Reduce (simplify) the answer if necessary.

$$3 \cdot 2\tfrac{1}{3} = \tfrac{3}{1} \cdot \tfrac{7}{3} = \tfrac{21}{3} = 7$$

$$1\tfrac{3}{4} \cdot 6 = \tfrac{7}{4} \cdot \tfrac{6}{1} = \tfrac{42}{4} = 10\tfrac{2}{4} {\scriptstyle \div \tfrac{2}{2}} = 10\tfrac{1}{2}$$

Ninth

One of nine equal parts.

$^4/_9$ is shown.

Numerator

The number that is written above the line in a fraction. It tells how many parts of the whole are being considered.

Example:

$\dfrac{6}{8}$ ⟵——— **6** is the numerator

Percent (%)

One-hundredth or 1 out of 100 parts. A fractional number with a denominator of 100.

Example:
20% is equal to 20 out of 100.

1. To find a percent, write the number as a fraction.
2. Divide the numerator by the denominator.
3. Multiply the answer by 100.

Percent (%), continued

I have 17 out of 32. What percent of the whole is that?

$$^{17}/_{32} = 32\overline{)17.00} \quad .53 \times 100 = \textbf{53\%}$$
$$\begin{array}{r} .53 \\ 32\overline{)17.00} \\ -160 \\ \hline 100 \\ -96 \\ \hline 4 \end{array}$$

Place Value

The value given to a digit because of the place it has in the numeral. In decimal numbers, all places are fractions with denominators that are powers of 10, such as 10, 100, and 1,000.

Examples:

$$.5 = {}^5\!/_{10} \quad .56 = {}^{56}\!/_{100} \quad .561 = {}^{561}\!/_{1,000} \quad .5617 = {}^{5,617}\!/_{10,000}$$

Proper Fraction

A fraction in which the numerator is smaller than the denominator. Proper fractions have a value less than 1.

Examples:

$${}^6\!/_7 \qquad \frac{2}{3}$$

Proportion

An equation that shows that two fractions are equal. These can be written in two ways.

Examples:

$$\frac{1}{2} = \frac{2}{4} \quad \text{or} \quad 1:2::2:4$$

Ratio

A comparison of two numbers by division. Ratios are commonly written as a fraction, although they may be written in other ways. The order in which the numbers are written is important: 1:4 is not the same as 4:1.

Examples:

$$\frac{3}{4} \qquad {}^3\!/_4 \qquad 3:4 \qquad 3 \text{ of } 4$$

Reciprocal

A number that gives a product of 1 when multiplied by the original number. To find the reciprocal of a number, switch the denominator and the numerator.

Examples:

$$\frac{4}{3} \text{ is the reciprocal of } \frac{3}{4} \text{ because } \frac{4}{3} \times \frac{3}{4} = \frac{12}{12} = 1$$

$$\frac{1}{5} \text{ is the reciprocal of } 5 \text{ because } \frac{1}{5} \times \frac{5}{1} = \frac{5}{5} = 1$$

Reducing Fractions

Reducing fractions is also commonly called simplifying and finding the lowest terms. Regardless of which term is used, to reduce a fraction one must find a factor of both numbers. There are two common methods to reduce (simplify) a fraction to its lowest terms.

✪ Method 1: Use Common Factors

Find the greatest common factor of the numerator and denominator, and then divide both numbers by the factor.

Example:
1, 3, 5, and 15 are common factors of 15 and 45. The greatest common factor is **15**, so divide the numerator and denominator by 15.

$$\frac{15}{45} \div \frac{15}{15} = \frac{1}{3}$$

$\frac{15}{45}$ in lowest terms is $\frac{1}{3}$.

✪ Method 2: Use Prime Factorizations

1. Write the prime factors of each number next to the numerator and denominator.
2. Leave both of the ones alone, but cross off any other factors they have in common.
3. Multiply the numbers on each row to produce a new fraction.
4. The fraction is now in lowest terms.

Reducing Fractions, continued
✪ Method 2: Use Prime Factorizations, continued

$$\frac{14}{26} = \frac{1,\cancel{2},7}{1,\cancel{2},13} = \frac{1 \times 7}{1 \times 13} = \frac{7}{13}$$

$$\frac{6}{8} = \frac{1,\cancel{2},3}{1,\cancel{2},2,2} = \frac{1 \times 3}{1 \times 2 \times 2} = \frac{3}{4}$$

Repeating Decimal

A decimal in which one digit, or a series of digits, is repeated over and over again, such as .3333 . . . or .212121. . . . Repeating decimals can be shown in the answer to a problem by using a bar over the first repeating series, such as $.\overline{3}$ or $.7\overline{63}$.

Seventh

One of seven equal parts.

$^5/_7$ is shown.

Sixth

One of six equal parts.

$^2/_6$ is shown.

Subtracting Decimals

1. Line up the decimal points so that the place value is in line.
2. Subtract as normal. Zeros can be added after the decimal point in order to make subtracting easier, and it won't change the answer.
3. Bring the decimal point straight down into the answer.

$$45.9 - 2.53 = \longrightarrow \begin{array}{r} \overset{8\ 10}{45.\cancel{9}0} \\ -2.53 \\ \hline 43.37 \end{array}$$

Subtracting Fractions

To subtract fractions, first look at the denominators.

Subtracting Fractions, continued

✪ Same Denominators

1. Leave the denominator the same, and write it in your answer.
2. Subtract the numerators.
3. Write the difference over the denominator.
4. Reduce (simplify) if needed.

$$\tfrac{7}{12} - \tfrac{4}{12} = \tfrac{3}{12} \div \tfrac{3}{3} = \tfrac{1}{4} \qquad \tfrac{3}{7} - \tfrac{2}{7} = \tfrac{1}{7}$$

✪ Different Denominators

1. Find a common denominator.
2. Make equivalent fractions.
3. Subtract the numerators.
4. Write the answer over the denominator.
5. Reduce (simplify) if needed.

$$\tfrac{2}{7} \times \tfrac{3}{3} = \tfrac{6}{21} \qquad\qquad \tfrac{1}{2} \times \tfrac{3}{3} = \tfrac{3}{6}$$
$$-\tfrac{3}{21} \quad = \tfrac{3}{21} \qquad\qquad -\tfrac{1}{3} \times \tfrac{2}{2} = \tfrac{2}{6}$$
$$\tfrac{3}{21} \div \tfrac{3}{3} = \tfrac{1}{7} \qquad\qquad \tfrac{1}{6}$$

Tenth
One of 10 equal parts.

$^1/_{10}$ is shown.

Terminating Decimal
A nonrepeating decimal with a limited and fixed number of digits.

Examples:
7.25
5.21
8.36

Third
One of three equal parts.

$^2/_3$ is shown.

Twelfth
One of 12 equal parts.

$^5/_{12}$ is shown.

Statistics and Probability

Average

A number that represents the middle or most normal of a set of numbers. Also called the mean or arithmetic mean.

> To find the average (mean):
> 1. Add all of the numbers together.
> 2. Divide by the number of items that were added together.
>
> Examples:
> 3, 5, 5, 11
> $3 + 5 + 5 + 11 = 24$ Four numbers were added, so divide 24 by 4.
> $24 \div 4 = 6$ The average (mean) is **6**.
>
> 6, 8, 14, 11, 7
> $$\frac{6 + 8 + 14 + 11 + 7}{5} = \frac{46}{5}$$ As $46 \div 5 = 9$ with a remainder of 1, the average (mean) is about 9.

Axes

Plural of axis.

Axis

One of the perpendicular lines that is used to form a graph. The x-axis (abscissa) is the horizontal axis, and the y-axis (ordinate) is the vertical axis. Together these form the basis of a coordinate plane, as in a coordinate graph.

Coordinate Graphing

A method that uses ordered pairs plotted on axis lines to locate specific points in a two-dimensional plane. See *Geometry—Coordinates*.

Data

Facts or figures from which conclusions can be formed. Factual information.

Dependent Event

An event whose outcome is affected by another event's outcome.

Event

Something that happens. The set of results or outcomes.

Extrapolate

To estimate a value beyond the known range of data by extending the known relationship or number pattern. To draw a conclusion based on known data.

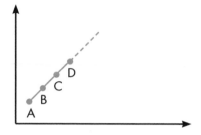

Frequency

How often something happens in a given time. The number of times an event, action, value, or characteristic occurs.

Graph

A picture that shows information in an organized way. To be complete, a graph needs a title, subtitle, labeled axes, and key (when appropriate).

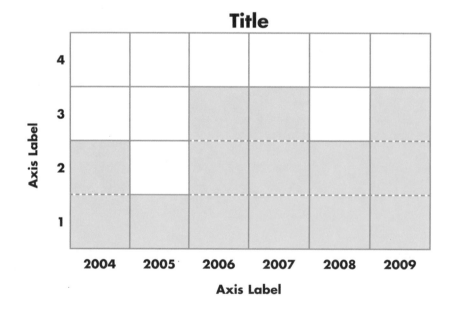

Graph, continued

✪ Bar Graph
A graph that shows information using bars.

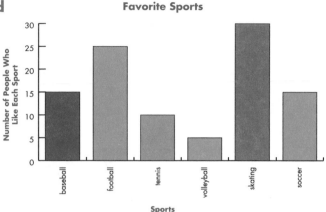

Favorite Sports

✪ Circle Graph (Pie Graph)
A graph that shows all data as a percentage or part of a circle.

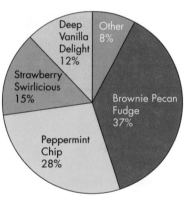

Favorite Flavors of Ice Cream

✪ Glyph
A type of pictograph that uses symbols to represent information. These are used to collect and interpret data.

Key

Eyes:
- Winter is your favorite season: two black eyes
- Winter is OK: one black and one closed eye
- You prefer another season: two closed eyes

Mouth:
- Prefer to go sledding: mouth drawn as smile
- Prefer to play hockey: mouth drawn as circle

Tie:
- Will watch part of the winter Olympics: striped
- Won't watch the winter Olympics: solid

Graph, continued

✪ Histogram

A special kind of bar graph that shows how frequently data occurs. The data are usually collected in a frequency table and then put into graph form. In a histogram, the adjacent bars are touching.

Total Number of Students by Age in Our School

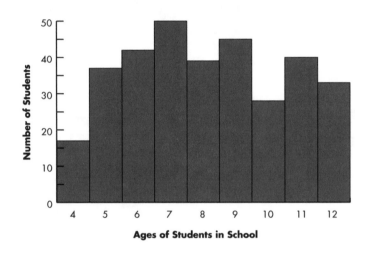

✪ Line Graph

A graph that shows information using lines. These are useful for comparing two or more things.

Amount of Candy Based on Bag Size

Graph, continued

✪ Picture Graph

A graph that uses pictures to show quantities.

Total Number of Pets

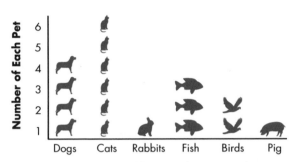

Number of Each Pet

6 5 4 3 2 1

Dogs   Cats   Rabbits   Fish   Birds   Pig

Pets Owned by People in Our Class

Independent Event

An event whose outcome does not affect the outcome of other events.

Interpolate

To estimate a value that is between two known values on a graph.

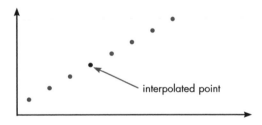

interpolated point

Interval

The amount of space or time between two things or events. The set of numbers between two given numbers or points.

Mean

The average value of a set of numbers.

To find the mean (average):
1.   Add all of the numbers together.
2.   Divide by the number of items that were added together.

Statistics and Probability

Mean, continued

Examples:
7, 9, 3, 14
7 + 9 + 3 + 14 = 33   Four numbers were added, so divide 33 by 4.

33 ÷ 4 = 8 r 1   The mean (average) is about **8**.

3, 9, 11, 13, 14

$$\frac{3+9+11+13+14}{5} = \frac{50}{5} = 10$$ The mean (average) is **10**.

Median

The number that would fall in the middle if the results were arranged in order from least to greatest (smallest to largest).

Examples:

80   85   87   92   93

median (87)

1   2   3   4   5   6   7   8   9   10

median (5.5)

Mode

The number that occurs most frequently in a set of information. When collecting data or information, it's the number of which there is the most.

Example:
5, 6, 7, 7, 9, 11   **7** is the mode.

Odds

The chances, written numerically, that something will or will not happen. These are written as ratios that compare the likelihood of events.

○ Odds Against

The likelihood that something won't happen.

$$\frac{\text{number of chances against}}{\text{number of chances for}}$$

Odds, continued

✪ Odds in Favor

The likelihood that something will happen.

$$\frac{\text{number of chances for}}{\text{number of chances against}}$$

Outcome

A possible result given a set of circumstances.

Percent (%)

One-hundredth or 1 out of 100 parts. A fractional number with a denominator of 100.

Example:

15% means $\frac{15}{100}$ or 0.15

Probability

The chance that something will or will not happen.

Random

All items in the set of information or data have an equal chance of happening or not happening with a certain frequency.

Random Sample

A small portion of a larger population that is selected in such a way that all selections have an equal probability of being chosen. The sample is used as a good representation of the whole population.

Range

The difference between the smallest number and the largest number in the sample.

Examples:
- If the lowest number in the sample is 13 and the highest number is 47, the range is the difference between the two. The range is 47 − 13 = **34**.
- {3, 15, 18, 27, 39}   The range is 39 − 3 = **36**.

Ratio

A comparison of two numbers by division. Ratios are commonly written as a fraction, although they may be written in other ways. The order in which the numbers are written is important; 1:4 is not the same as 4:1.

Examples:
1 to 2   1:2   ½

Sample

A part of something used to represent the whole group. Samples can be used to make predictions about the larger group.

Slope

A number used to describe the steepness of a straight line. The larger the slope, the steeper the line. If the line is level, there is no slope and it is written as zero (0). If the line goes up, it has a positive slope. If the line goes down it has a negative slope. Slope is used in algebra, geometry, calculus, and trigonometry, and is represented through coordinate graphing.

Statistics

Numerical facts or data that can be put together or tabulated to present information about a given subject.

Stem-and-Leaf Plot

A method of categorizing numerical data so that the shape of the distribution easily can be seen. A way of looking at the range of data and its frequency.

Example:
Ages of people in the family:

11	15		
23	24	29	29
31	38	38	
44	47		
56	57		

tens	ones
1	1 5
2	3 4 9 9
3	1 8 8
4	4 7
5	6 7

Survey

A way to gather data
or opinions from a sample.

Favorite Lunch Choices at School

Pizza	ЖЖ IIII
Hot Dogs	ЖЖ
Hamburgers	II
Chicken Nuggets	ЖЖ III

Tally Marks

A set of five lines used to keep
track of the number of something
when counting. In the United
States, Canada, and European
countries, these are written as
four vertical lines crossed by a
diagonal line.

In Asian countries and elsewhere,
this mark is shown as the tally
symbol.

Problem Solving

Algorithm

Any special method of solving a problem.

Attribute

A characteristic, property, or quality of something that is useful in classifying.

Characteristic

A quality, attribute, or property of something that is useful in classifying.

Classify

To arrange or group something into categories according to some rule or common characteristic.

Combination

Any arrangement of elements with no consideration for the order of the elements.

Examples:
* The combinations of the letters A, B, C, and D, taken three at a time, are ABC, ABD, ACD, and BCD.
* The combinations of the letters A, B, C, and D, taken two at a time, are AB, AC, AD, BC, BD, and CD.

Disjoint Sets

Sets that have no members in common.

Example:
Z = {p, q, r}
Y = {d, e, f}
$Z \cap Y = \varnothing$

Empty Set

A set that has no elements, shown by using the symbol $\varnothing$.

Estimate

To do quick, mental calculations (often using rounding) to get an approximate answer.

Example:
$$\begin{array}{r} 57 \\ \times\ 5 \\ \hline \end{array} \rightarrow \begin{array}{r} 60 \\ \times\ 5 \\ \hline \end{array}$$

The answer should be around 300.

Information

✪ Given Information

The information presented in the problem.

✪ Extraneous Information

Information in the problem that is not necessary or relevant to solve it. Extra information.

✪ Necessary Information

Information in the problem that must be used to solve the problem.

Intersection

A set of elements that is common to two sets, shown by the symbol ∩.

Examples:
$\{2, 4, 6, 8, 12\} \cap \{3, 6, 9, 12, 15\} = \{6, 12\}$

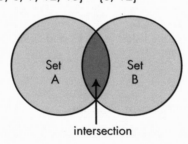

intersection

Inverse

The opposite.

Example:
Multiplication is the inverse of division.

Mapping

An operation that matches the members of one set with the members of another set in such a way that the pairs are uniquely paired.

Example:
Set 1   Set 2
4   ⟶   7
7   ⟶   10
12   ⟶   15
22   ⟶   25

In this relationship, 12 maps to 15, and 15 is the image of 12.

One-to-One Correspondence

A matching of every element in one set to a unique element in another set.

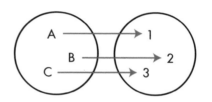

Pattern

A regular event, happening, or arrangement of numbers, objects, or occurrences.

Permutation

Any of the different ordered combinations possible with a given set of elements.

Example:
The permutations of the numbers 1, 2, and 3 are:
{1, 2, 3} {1, 3, 2} {2, 1, 3} {2, 3, 1} {3, 1, 2} {3, 2, 1}

Property

A characteristic, attribute, or quality of something that is useful in classifying.

Rule

A method used for solving a problem.

Set

A group of things that share some quality in common. A collection or group of numbers or other objects that follow a pattern or rule, have a common characteristic, or are the solutions to a problem. Sets are shown with the use of braces { }.

Examples:

{2, 4, 6, 8}   {10, 20, 30, 40, . . .}

{crab, lobster, shrimp, barnacle}   {1/2, 2/4, 3/6, 4/8, . . .}

H = {Cinco de Mayo, Mother's Day, Memorial Day}

H = {Holidays in May}

Steps for Successful Problem Solving

1. Read the problem.
2. Find the question asked or problem to be solved.
3. Decide on a problem-solving strategy.
4. Solve, using a problem-solving strategy.
5. Reread the problem and recheck your work to make sure you answered the question correctly.

Strategy

A plan of action used to solve a problem. There are many different strategies that can be used to solve problems.

Examples:

- Act out or use objects
- Brainstorm for multiple answers
- Classify
- Draw a picture
- Eliminate possibilities
- Guess and check (also called trial and error)
- Make a simple problem
- Make an organized list
- Use a pattern
- Use logical reasoning
- Use multiple steps
- Use or make a table, chart, or diagram
- Work backward

Subset

A set that is part of another set. It is shown with the symbol ⊂.

Example:
{1, 3, 5, 7} is a subset of {1, 2, 3, 4, 5, 6, 7, 8}
{1, 3, 5, 7} ⊂ {1, 2, 3, 4, 5, 6, 7, 8}

Table

A systematic arrangement of data.

Union

A set of elements, shown by using the symbol ∪, that is the sum of all of the elements in one set and all of the elements in another set.

Examples:
{1, 3, 5, 6} ∪ {2, 4, 6} = {1, 2, 3, 4, 5, 6}

J = {red, yellow, orange}
M = {blue, green, violet}
J ∪ M = {red, yellow, orange, blue, green, violet}

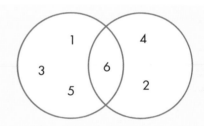

Venn Diagram

Diagrams in which intersecting circles are used to represent different sets of elements. A way to show similarities and differences and compare information.

Examples:

Quick Reference Guides

Quick Reference Guide: Decimals

Adding Decimals

1. Line up the decimal points so that the place value is in line.
2. Add as normal. Zeros can be added after the decimal point in order to make adding easier, and it won't change the answer.
3. Bring the decimal point straight down into the answer.

$5 + .34 + 2.738 =$	$.83 + 4.2 =$	$9 + 6 + .34 =$
5.000	.83	.90
.340	+ 4.20	6.00
+ 2.738	5.03	+ .34
8.078		7.24

Comparing Decimals

To determine which decimal is larger or smaller, place value must be compared.

1. Line up the decimal points.
2. Compare tenths, then hundredths, and then thousandths.

.6 ___ .19 means the same as .60 ___ .19

.6
.19 ⟶ 6 tenths is larger than 1 tenth

1. Line up decimal points.   0.56
                                 0.324

2. Look at place value: 5 tenths is larger than 3 tenths, so **0.56** is larger than **0.324**.

Converting Decimals

✪ Decimal to Fraction

To change a decimal to a fraction, use place value.

1. Decide whether the decimal represents tenths, hundredths, thousandths, etc.
2. Write the numerical part of the decimal over the appropriate power of 10—over 10 if the decimal was in the tenths place, over 100 if the decimal was in the hundredths place, and so on.

Math Dictionary for Kids

Converting Decimals, continued

✪ Decimal to Fraction, continued

3. Reduce the fraction.

Example: .05 is 5 hundredths	$\dfrac{5}{100}$	$\dfrac{5}{100} \div \dfrac{5}{5} = \dfrac{1}{20}$

✪ Decimal to Percent

To change a decimal to a percent, move the decimal point.
1. Move the decimal point two places to the right.
2. Add a percent sign (%).
3. Add zeros for placeholders if necessary.

Examples:
.72 = 72%   .8 = 80%
.523 = 52.3%   .09 = 9%

✪ Fraction to Decimal

To find the decimal for a fraction: $^3/_8$

1. Divide the numerator by the denominator

$$8\overline{)3}$$

2. Add a decimal point and zeros to the dividend. Bring the decimal point straight up to the quotient.

$$8\overline{)3.00}$$

3. Divide as normal; write the answer with the decimal point.

$$
\begin{array}{r}
.375 \\
8{\overline{)3.00}} \\
-2\ 4 \\
\hline
60 \\
-5\ 6 \\
\hline
40 \\
-40 \\
\hline
0
\end{array}
$$

114

Dividing Decimals

1. Write the problem as normal.
2. Bring the decimal point straight up.
3. Divide as normal.

```
       1.57
    4) 6.28
      -4
       22
      -20
        28
       -28
         0
```

Multiplying Decimals

1. Write and solve the problem as normal.
2. Count the total number of places after each decimal in the numbers being multiplied.
3. Position the decimal the same number of places in the answer.

```
      3.15
    × 2.7
     2205
   +6300
    8.505
```

Subtracting Decimals

1. Line up the decimal points so that the place value is in line.
2. Subtract as normal. Zeros can be added after the decimal point in order to make subtracting easier, and it won't change the answer.
3. Bring the decimal point straight down into the answer.

```
     7  2 10
    6 8. 3 0
    - 4. 6 9
    6 3. 6 1
```

Quick Reference Guide: Division

Algorithm Division

1. Write a multiples table for the divisor.
2. Start with the first digit in the dividend. Can it be divided by the divisor? If not, hold the place with a zero.
3. Look at the first two digits. Can they be divided? If so, check the multiples table to see how many times the divisor can be subtracted. Subtract it.
4. Continue in this way until you can divide no more and your remainder is smaller than the divisor.

```
    0            02            026
15)398        15)398        15)398
               -30           -30
                 9            98
                             -90
                               8
```

Answer: 26 r 8

Multiples Table for 15

1	15
2	30
3	45
4	60
5	75
6	90
7	105
8	120
9	135

Larger Numbers: Multiples Table

1. Make a multiples table for the number you are dividing by, the divisor.
2. Subtract the largest multiple of the divisor that does not exceed the dividend.
3. When you can't subtract any more multiples of 100s, begin subtracting multiples of 10s, and then multiples of 1 through 9.
4. When you can't subtract any more multiples, add the number of multiples that have been subtracted. This final number is the quotient.

Larger Numbers: Multiples Table, continued

Multiples Table for 53

1	53	11	583
2	106	20	1,060
3	159	30	1,590
4	212	40	2,120
5	265	50	2,650
6	318	60	3,180
7	371	70	3,710
8	424	80	4,240
9	477	90	4,770
10	530	100	5,300

$$
\begin{array}{r}
100+60+0 \\
53\overline{)8531} \\
-5300 \\
\hline
3231 \\
-3180 \\
\hline
51
\end{array}
$$

Answer: 160 r 51

Repeated Subtraction

15 was subtracted a total of five times with 4 remaining, so the answer is **5 r 4** or **5 ⁴/₁₅**.

$$
\begin{array}{r}
5\,r\,4 \\
15\overline{)79} \\
-15 \\
\hline
^5\!\!\!\!64 \\
-15 \\
\hline
49 \\
-15 \\
\hline
^2\!\!\!\!34 \\
-15 \\
\hline
19 \\
-15 \\
\hline
4
\end{array}
$$

Quick Reference
Guide: Division

Math Dictionary for Kids

Use Manipulatives

Use beans, counters, or other objects, or draw a picture. Count out the number of beans that need to be divided. Divide them equally into the number of groups that are you are dividing by.

61 ÷ 9 = 6 r 7

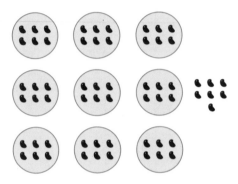

Use tiles or paper squares. Count out the number of tiles that need to be divided. Put them into the number of rows you are dividing by. Count the number of columns you are about to make, and then count the remainder.

25 ÷ 4 = 6 r 1

Quick Reference Guide: Fractions

Adding Fractions

To add fractions, first look at the denominators.

✪ Same Denominators
1. Leave the denominator the same, and write it in your answer.
2. Add the numerators.
3. Write the sum over the denominator.
4. Reduce (simplify) if needed.

$$\frac{3}{8}+\frac{4}{8}=\frac{7}{8} \qquad \frac{4}{5}+\frac{1}{5}=\frac{5}{5}=1 \qquad \frac{1}{4}+\frac{2}{4}=\frac{3}{4}$$

✪ Different Denominators
1. Find a common denominator.
2. Make equivalent fractions.
3. Add the numerators.
4. Write the sum over the common denominator.
5. Reduce (simplify) if needed.

$$
\begin{array}{l}
\frac{1}{6}\times\frac{3}{3}=\frac{3}{18} \\[4pt]
+\frac{4}{18} \quad =\frac{4}{18} \\[2pt]
\hline
\frac{7}{18}
\end{array}
\qquad
\begin{array}{l}
\frac{3}{5}\times\frac{3}{3}=\frac{9}{15} \\[4pt]
+\frac{1}{3}\times\frac{5}{5}=\frac{5}{15} \\[2pt]
\hline
\frac{14}{15}
\end{array}
$$

Comparing Fractions

There are several ways to compare fractions.

✪ Find a Common Denominator

Find a common denominator for both fractions, and then compare the two fractions to determine which is larger.

Which is larger, $\frac{5}{7}$ or $\frac{9}{10}$?

$$\frac{5}{7} \times \frac{10}{10} = \frac{50}{70} \qquad \frac{9}{10} \times \frac{7}{7} = \frac{63}{70}$$

$\frac{63}{70}$ is larger than $\frac{50}{70}$, so $\frac{9}{10}$ is larger than $\frac{5}{7}$.

Math Dictionary for Kids

✪ Cross Multiply
Multiply the numerator of one fraction by the denominator of the other. Repeat the process with the other two numbers, and compare the two products to determine which fraction is larger.

$$\frac{3}{4} \times \frac{2}{3}$$

$3 \times 3 = 9$
$4 \times 2 = 8$
9 is greater than 8, so ¾ is greater than ⅔.

✪ Convert Fractions to Decimals
Write each fraction as a division problem, divide to find the decimals, and then compare the decimal numbers to determine which is larger.

$$\frac{5}{6} \underline{\quad} \frac{1}{2}$$

```
     .83              .5
6)⁴5.¹00          2)1.0
  -4 8             -10
    20               0
  - 18
     2
```

.83 is greater than .5, so $\frac{5}{6}$ is greater than $\frac{1}{2}$.

Converting Fractions
✪ Fraction to Decimal
To find the decimal for a fraction, divide: ³⁄₅

1. Divide the numerator by the denominator.

   $5)\overline{3}$

2. Add a decimal point and zeros to the dividend. Bring the decimal point straight up to the quotient.

   $5)\overline{3.00}$

✪ Fraction to Decimal, continued

3. Divide as normal, and then write the answer with the decimal point.

$$\begin{array}{r} .6 \\ 5\overline{)\,3.0} \\ -3\,0 \\ \hline 0 \end{array}$$

✪ Improper Fraction to Mixed or Whole Number

To convert an improper fraction to a mixed or whole number, use division.

1. Divide the numerator by the denominator.
2. Write the remainder as a fraction.

$$\frac{32}{9} \rightarrow 9\overline{)32} \rightarrow 9\overline{)\,{}^2\!3\,{}^1\!2} \rightarrow 3\,\tfrac{5}{9}$$
$$\begin{array}{r} 3 \\ -2\,7 \\ \hline 5 \end{array}$$

✪ Mixed Number to Improper Fraction

To convert a mixed number to an improper fraction, use multiplication.

1. Multiply the denominator by the whole number.
2. Add the numerator to the answer.
3. Put the answer over the original denominator.

$$4\frac{2}{3} = 4\frac{^+2}{_\times 3} = \frac{14}{3} \quad \text{or} \quad 4\frac{2}{3} = \frac{(4\times3)+2}{3} = \frac{14}{3}$$

3 x 4 = 12
12 + 2 = 14
¹⁴⁄₁₃

3 x 4 + 2
The denominator stays the same.

To find a common denominator of two or more fractions, make lists of multiples.

Example:
⅔   Multiples of 3:   3   6   **9**   12   15   **18**   21   24   **27**   30   33
⅝   Multiples of 9:   **9**   **18**   **27**   36   45   54   63   72   81   90   99

9, 18, and 27 are multiples of 3 and 9, so **9**, **18**, and **27** are common denominators of ⅔ and ⅝.

Math Dictionary for Kids

Common Denominators, continued

Using 9 as a common denominator, multiply both the numerator and denominator of one fraction by the number needed to produce a denominator of 9. Repeat for the second fraction. The numbers by which the fractions are multiplied will usually be different for each fraction.

$$\frac{2}{3} \times \frac{3}{3} = \frac{6}{9}$$

$$\frac{5}{9} \times \frac{1}{1} = \frac{5}{9}$$

Now that the fractions have a common denominator, they can be compared, added, or subtracted easily.

Sometimes you will only need to adjust one of the fractions.

$$\frac{1}{2} \times \frac{4}{4} = \frac{4}{8}$$

The fractions now can be compared, added, or subtracted.

$$\frac{3}{8}$$

Dividing Fractions

When fractions are divided, a reciprocal and multiplication must be used. To find a fraction's reciprocal, invert the fraction by writing the numerator on the bottom and the denominator on the top. After the fraction has been inverted, multiply the two fractions together.

✪ **To divide regular fractions:**
1. Invert the divisor it to find the reciprocal.
2. Multiply the numerators.
3. Multiply the denominators.
4. Change the answer to a mixed or whole number.
5. Reduce (simplify) the answer if necessary.

$$\frac{3}{7} \div \frac{4}{5} = \frac{3}{7} \cdot \frac{5}{4} = \frac{15}{28}$$

✪ **To divide improper fractions:**
1. Invert the divisor.
2. Multiply the numerators.
3. Multiply the denominators.
4. Change the answer to a mixed or whole number.

Dividing Fractions, continued

✪ To divide improper fractions, continued

5. Reduce (simplify) the answer if necessary.

$$\frac{8}{3} \div \frac{4}{2} = \frac{8}{3} \cdot \frac{2}{4} = \frac{16}{12} = 1\frac{4}{12} \div \frac{4}{4} = 1\frac{1}{3}$$

✪ To divide fractions with mixed numbers:

1. Change any mixed numbers to improper fractions.
2. Invert the divisor.
3. Multiply the numerators.
4. Multiply the denominators.
5. Change the answer to a mixed or whole number.
6. Reduce (simplify) the answer if necessary.

$$3\frac{1}{3} \div 2\frac{3}{5} = \frac{10}{3} \div \frac{13}{5} = \frac{10}{3} \cdot \frac{5}{13} = \frac{50}{39} = 1\frac{11}{39}$$

✪ To divide fractions and whole numbers:

1. Change any whole number to its fractional equivalent.
2. Invert the divisor.
3. Multiply the numerators.
4. Multiply the denominators.
5. Change the answer to a mixed or whole number.
6. Reduce (simplify) the answer if necessary.

$$5 \div \frac{2}{3} = \frac{5}{1} \div \frac{2}{3} = \frac{5}{1} \cdot \frac{3}{2} = \frac{15}{2} = 7\frac{1}{2}$$

Finding Equivalent Fractions

There are several ways to find equivalent fractions.

✪ Multiply or Divide

Multiply or divide both the numerator and the denominator by the same number.

$$\frac{2}{7} \times \frac{3}{3} = \frac{6}{21} \qquad \frac{9}{10} \times \frac{2}{2} = \frac{18}{20}$$

$$\frac{30}{36} \div \frac{6}{6} = \frac{5}{6} \qquad \frac{5}{15} \div \frac{5}{5} = \frac{1}{3}$$

Finding Equivalent Fractions, continued

✪ Use Multiples

List the multiples for the numbers in the numerator and denominator in two separate rows. The numbers in the top row become the numerators in the equivalent fractions, while the numbers in the bottom rows become the denominators.

$$\frac{4}{5} = \begin{array}{ccccccccc} 4 & 8 & 12 & 16 & 20 & 24 & 28 & 32 & 36 \\ 5 & 10 & 15 & 20 & 25 & 30 & 35 & 40 & 45 \end{array}$$

Fractions equivalent to ⅘ are: ⁸⁄₁₀, ¹²⁄₁₅, ¹⁶⁄₂₀, ²⁰⁄₂₅, ²⁴⁄₃₀, ²⁸⁄₃₅, ³²⁄₄₀, ³⁶⁄₄₅

Finding a Fraction of a Number

There are two methods for finding a fraction (part) of a number.

✪ Draw It Out

¾ of 40 = 30   Break 40 into 4 groups, then look at 3 of them.

40

★★★★★★★★★★ ★★★★★★★★★★ ★★★★★★★★★★ ☆☆☆☆☆☆☆☆☆☆

30

✪ Use Division and Multiplication

1. Divide the whole number by the fraction's denominator.
2. Multiply the answer by the numerator.

Examples:
⅘ of 30

1. Divide the whole number by the denominator to find one fractional part.
   30 ÷ 5 = 6
2. Multiply the answer by the numerator of the fraction. This finds the number of fractional parts.
3. ⅘ of 30 = 24   24 is ⅘ of 30.

⁴⁄₇ of 49
- 49 ÷ 7 = 7
- 7 x 4 = 28
- 28 is ⁴⁄₇ of 49

$\frac{2}{3}$ of 18   3)18   6 × 2 = 12

Multiplying Fractions

The steps taken to multiply fractions depends on the type of fraction in the problem.

✪ To multiply regular fractions:
1. Multiply the numerators.
2. Multiply the denominators.
3. Reduce (simplify) the answer if necessary.

$$\frac{1}{4}\cdot\frac{3}{7}=\frac{3}{28}\qquad\frac{2}{8}\cdot\frac{4}{6}=\frac{8}{48}\div\frac{8}{8}=\frac{1}{6}$$

✪ To multiply improper fractions:
1. Multiply the numerators.
2. Multiply the denominators.
3. Change the answer to a mixed or whole number.
4. Reduce (simplify) the answer if necessary.

$$\frac{5}{3}\cdot\frac{4}{2}=\frac{20}{6}=3\frac{2}{6}\div\frac{2}{2}=3\frac{1}{3}$$

✪ To multiply fractions with mixed numbers:
1. Change any mixed numbers to improper fractions.
2. Multiply the numerators.
3. Multiply the denominators.
4. Change the answer to a mixed or whole number.
5. Reduce (simplify) the answer if necessary.

$$1\frac{1}{3}\cdot2\frac{1}{5}=\frac{4}{3}\cdot\frac{11}{5}=\frac{44}{15}=2\frac{14}{15}$$

✪ To multiply fractions with whole numbers:
1. Change any whole number to its fractional equivalent.
2. Multiply the numerators.
3. Multiply the denominators.
4. Change the answer to a mixed or whole number.
5. Reduce (simplify) the answer if necessary.

$$1\frac{1}{3}\cdot2=\frac{4}{3}\cdot\frac{2}{1}=\frac{8}{3}=2\frac{2}{3}$$

Math Dictionary for Kids

Reducing Fractions

There are two common ways to reduce (simplify) a fraction to lowest terms.

✪ Use Common Factors

Find the greatest common factor of the numerator and denominator, and then divide both numbers by the factor.

$^{18}/_{27}$

1, 3, and 9 are common factors of 18 and 27. The greatest common factor is **9**, so divide the numerator and denominator by 9.

$$\frac{18}{27} \div \frac{9}{9} = \frac{2}{3}$$

$\frac{18}{27}$ in lowest terms is $\frac{2}{3}$.

✪ Use Prime Factorizations

1. Write the prime factors of each number next to the numerator and denominator.
2. Leave both of the ones alone, but cross off any other factors they have in common.
3. Multiply the numbers on each row to produce a new fraction.
4. The fraction is now in lowest terms.

$$\frac{4}{14} = \frac{1,\cancel{2},2}{1,\cancel{2},7} = \frac{1 \times 2}{1 \times 7} = \frac{2}{7}$$

Subtracting Fractions

To subtract fractions, first look at the denominators.

✪ Same Denominators

1. Leave the denominator the same, and write it in your answer.
2. Subtract the numerators.
3. Write the difference over the denominator.
4. Reduce (simplify) if needed.

$$^{7}/_{9} - ^{4}/_{9} = ^{3}/_{9} \div ^{3}/_{3} = ^{1}/_{3} \qquad ^{4}/_{5} - ^{3}/_{5} = ^{1}/_{5}$$

Subtracting Fractions, continued

✪ Different Denominators

1. Find a common denominator.
2. Make equivalent fractions.
3. Subtract the numerators.
4. Write the answer over the denominator.
5. Reduce (simplify) if needed.

$$\frac{3}{8} \times \frac{3}{3} = \frac{9}{24}$$
$$-\frac{1}{24} \quad = \frac{1}{24}$$
$$\overline{\frac{8}{24} \div \frac{8}{8} = \frac{1}{3}}$$

$$\frac{3}{5} \times \frac{2}{2} = \frac{6}{10}$$
$$-\frac{1}{2} \times \frac{5}{5} = \frac{5}{10}$$
$$\overline{\frac{1}{10}}$$

Quick Reference Guide: Multiplication

Algorithm Multiplication

1. Start with the ones place. Multiply every number on top by that number.

    $$
    \begin{array}{r}
    367 \\
    \times\ 24 \\
    \hline
    \end{array}
    $$

    3 2 1

    Step 1: $4 \times 7 = 28$
    Step 2: $4 \times 6 = 24$
    Step 3: $4 \times 3 = 12$

    $$
    \begin{array}{r}
    ^{2\ 2}367 \\
    \times\ 24 \\
    \hline
    1468 \\
    \end{array}
    $$

2. Once you've multiplied every digit on the top by the number in the one's place:
    - cross off any numbers you've carried so you don't get confused, and
    - circle the number in the ones place to show that you've used it, and bring that zero straight down to show that you've used it. It's going to hold your place.

    $$
    \begin{array}{r}
    ^{\not2\ \not2}367 \\
    \times\ 2\,④ \\
    \hline
    1468 \\
    0 \\
    \end{array}
    $$

3. Move to the tens place. Multiply every number on the top by the digit in the tens place.

    $$
    \begin{array}{r}
    ^{\not2\ \not2}367 \\
    \times\ 2\,④ \\
    \hline
    1468 \\
    0 \\
    \end{array}
    $$

    6 5 4

    Step 4: $2 \times 7 = 14$
    Step 5: $2 \times 6 = 12$
    Step 6: $2 \times 3 = 6$

    $$
    \begin{array}{r}
    ^{1\ 1}_{\not2\ \not2}367 \\
    \times\ 2\,④ \\
    \hline
    1468 \\
    7340 \\
    \end{array}
    $$

4. Add what you've recorded below to get your final answer.

    $$
    \begin{array}{r}
    ^{1\ 1}_{\not2\ \not2}367 \\
    \times\ 2\,④ \\
    \hline
    1468 \\
    +7340 \\
    \hline
    8808 \\
    \end{array}
    $$

Break Apart

Example:
6 x 12 =
3 x 12 = 36
3 x 12 = 36

36 + 36 = 72

Break Apart (Larger Numbers)

Example:

$$200 + 12 = 212$$

"Count By" Using Multiples

Example:
3 x 6 = 18
3 + 3 + 3 + 3 + 3 + 3 = 18
or 3 6 9 12 15 18

Crossed Lines (Count Intersections)

Example:

Draw a Picture

Example:
8 x 3 = 24

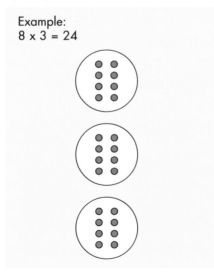

Window Pane Math

Example:
71 x 18 = 1,278

Quick Reference Guide: Percents

Converting Percents

✪ Decimal to Percent

To change a decimal to a percent:

1. Move the decimal point two places to the right.
2. Add a percent sign (%).
3. Add zeros for placeholders if necessary.

Examples:
.35 = 35%   .293 = 29.3%
.0 = 1%   .9 = 90%

✪ Percent to a Decimal

To change a percentage to a decimal, move the decimal point two places to the left. Add zeros as placeholders if necessary.

Examples:
68% = .68   14.3% = .143
6% = .06

Finding the Percent of a Given Number

1. To find a percent, write the numbers as a fraction (part over whole).
2. Divide the numerator by the denominator.
3. Multiply the answer by 100.

I have 9 out of 18. What percent of the whole is that?

$$\frac{9}{18} = 18\overline{)9.0} \quad .5 \times 100 = \mathbf{50\%}$$

$$\begin{array}{r} .5 \\ 18\overline{)9.0} \\ -90 \\ \hline 0 \end{array}$$

Finding the Number for a Given Percent

1. Change the percent to a decimal.
2. Multiply the decimal times the number.
3. Move the decimal point to the appropriate position in the answer.

Example:
What is 25% of 45?

```
   45
 ×.25
  225
  900
11.25
```

25% of 45 is **11.25**.

Learning With Manipulatives

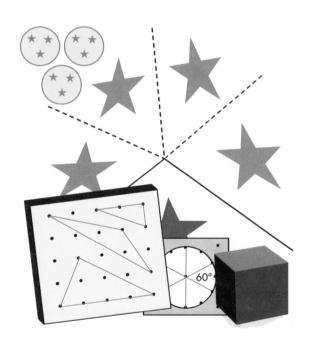

Learning With Manipulatives: Base 10s

Basic Fact Multiples

The rule when building multiplication problems with Base 10s, as with tiles, is that you have to build a perfect rectangle or square in order to find the answer.

1. Write the problem; build it with Base 10s.
2. Count the multiples by drawing the problem out on graph paper; write the number problem.
3. Record work on a blank 10 x 10 grid worksheet to make a multiplication chart.

Examples:
$5 \times 6 = 30$

					6
					12
					18
					24
					30

Look for patterns in multiples, and for the division/multiplication link.

Multiplying Basic Facts

This can be completed with either a Base-10 mat or with a piece of colored paper.

1. Build the problem outside of the markings on the mat (or off the edge of the colored paper).
2. Build the solution inside the mat (or on the paper).
3. Draw the problem and the solution on graph paper.
4. Write the answer on the grid in the drawing.
5. Write the problem and solution numerically.

In this example, the problem is built with Base-10 blocks on a Base-10 work mat.

Multiplying Basic Facts, continued

Example:
3 x 4 = 12

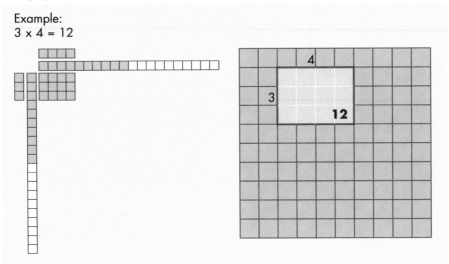

Multiplying Decimals

A Base-10 mat is made up of 100 little pieces, but is thought of as one whole piece.

1. Use unit blocks to cover the pieces, then think of money to record the answer. For example, if only 1 little square out of 100 is covered, that's like one penny, so it would be written as .01.

2. If the problem given is .4 times .6, cover 4 rows by 6 columns with unit cubes.

3. Count how many pieces are covered, and then think of money. For example, .4 x .6 has an area of .24. There are 24 units that cover it. That's like saying there are 24 out of 100 pennies, so .24 would be the answer.

Example:

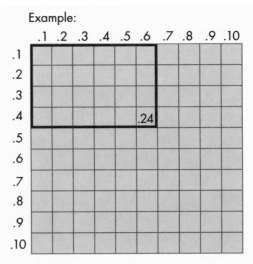

Multiplying Intermediate 2-Digit x 1-Digit Problems

This can be completed with either a Base-10 mat or with a piece of colored paper.

1. Build the problem outside of the markings on the mat (or off the edge of the colored paper).
2. Build the solution inside the mat (or on the paper).
3. Draw the problem and the solution on graph paper.
4. Write the answer on the grid in the drawing.
5. Write the problem and solution numerically.
6. Use a different-colored pencil to draw the problem and the solution.

Build It

Draw It

Write It

$$\begin{array}{r} 13 \\ \times\ 7 \\ \hline 70 \\ +\ 21 \\ \hline 91 \end{array}$$

Math Dictionary for Kids

Multiplying Intermediate 2-Digit x 2-Digit Problems

This can be done with either a Base-10 mat or with a piece of colored paper.

1. Build the problem outside of the markings on the mat (or off the edge of the colored paper).
2. Build the solution inside the mat (or on the paper).
3. Draw the problem and the solution on graph paper.
4. Write the answer on the grid in the drawing.
5. Write the problem and solution numerically.
6. Use a different-colored pencil to draw the problem and the solution.

Build It

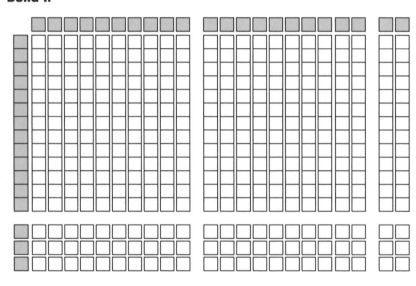

Multiplying Intermediate 2-Digit x 2-Digit Problems, continued

Draw It

Write It

```
   13
 x 21
 ────
  200
   80
 +  6
 ────
  286
```

Learning With Manipulatives: Geoboards

Angles and Triangles

Geoboards can be used to model the following:

★ acute, obtuse, right, and straight angles;

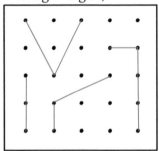

★ isosceles right triangles, isosceles acute triangles, and isosceles obtuse triangles; and

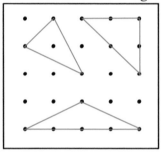

★ equilateral, isosceles, and scalene triangles;

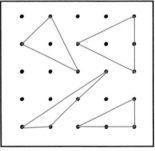

★ scalene right triangles, scalene acute triangles, and scalene obtuse triangles.

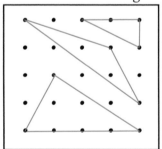

Angle Measurement

Many geoboards have the circumference of a circle outlined in pegs on the back of the board. Because every circle can be divided evenly into 360° degrees, geoboards can be used to find the measure of central angles.

To do this, use a calculator and this equation: 360 ÷ the number of same-sized angles built in the circle = the number of degrees in each angle.

360° divided into two even pieces:
360° ÷ 2 = 180°

360° divided into three even pieces:
360° ÷ 3 = 120°

360° divided into four even pieces:
360° ÷ 4 = 90°

360° divided into six even pieces:
360° ÷ 6 = 60°

360° ÷ 12 = 30°
(not pictured)

Learning With
Manipulatives:
Geoboards

Math Dictionary for Kids

Area: Irregular Polygons

Area of irregular polygons can be determined by breaking the shape into bits according how they make up a larger rectangle.

1. Build and draw the shape on dot paper.
2. Count whole squares first.
3. Then count halves.
4. Next, look at the remainder as part of a larger rectangle.
5. Label them on dot paper.
6. Add up the total.

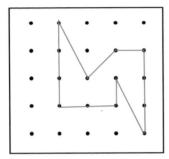

1. Build and draw the shape.

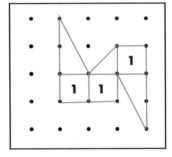

2. Count the whole squares.

3. Count the halves.

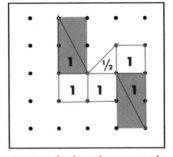

4. Next, look at the remainder as part of the rectangles they make up.

Example:
Two whole squares make up this rectangle, and half of that is used. This portion equals 1.

Area: Regular Polygons

Area of regular polygons can be determined by using the square units on the geoboard.

1. Identify the unit of measure.
2. Count the number of square units inside.
3. Don't forget to count halves.

A = 3

 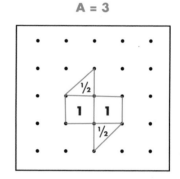

Building Polygons and Other Figures

Geoboards are useful tools to show geometric concepts. They come in a variety of pin sizes, from 5 x 5 to 11 x 11. Among other concepts, they are well suited to modeling and practicing with:

★ regular and irregular polygons;
★ angles;
★ triangles;
★ circumference, diameter, radius, and chords;
★ parallel, perpendicular, and intersecting lines; and
★ central angles and inscribed angles.

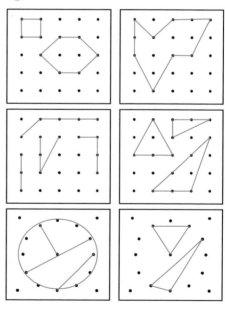

Math Dictionary for Kids

Circumference, Diameter, Radius, and Chord

Geoboards can be used to model the different parts of a circle.

★ **Circumference:** the distance around the circle.

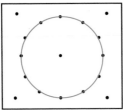

★ **Radius:** the distance from the center of the circle to a point on the circle.

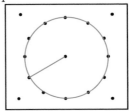

★ **Diameter:** a chord that passes through the center of the circle.

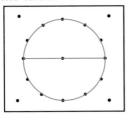

★ **Chord:** a line segment that connects two points on a circle.

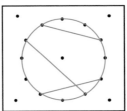

Fractions

Geoboards can be used to model fractions in several different ways.

1. Build the model; draw it on dot paper. Determine the fractional part by counting units.
2. Start with a model; draw it on dot paper. Divide it into an equal number of sections, according to the denominator.
3. Find as many ways possible to build a certain fraction. Use a variety; for example, build ⅓, then ⅚, then ⅖.

Example 1:

Example 2:

Fractions, continued

Example 3:

  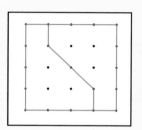

Many geoboards have the circumference of a circle outlined in pegs on the back of the board. These generally have 12 pegs, so the circle can be evenly divided into equal pieces. Each piece equals $\frac{1}{12}$, so that's the basis for conversion.

1. Write the problem on dot paper and label the fractional parts.
2. Make any necessary conversions.
3. Solve.
4. Reduce to lowest terms.

$\frac{1}{6} + \frac{1}{12} =$

$\frac{2}{12} + \frac{1}{12} = \frac{3}{12}$

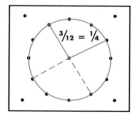

Reduce to lowest terms: $\frac{3}{12} = \frac{1}{4}$

Math Dictionary for Kids

Fraction Equivalence
1. Build a model of one whole.
2. Find one way to evenly divide it.
3. Name the fractional piece.
4. Build the model again.
5. Find another way to divide it.
6. Rename it.

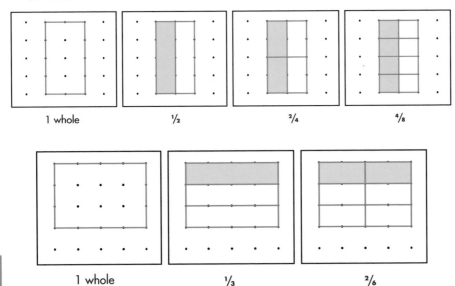

1 whole   ½   ²⁄₄   ⁴⁄₈

1 whole   ⅓   ²⁄₆

Multiplying Fractions
Geoboards can be used as a beginning step for multiplying simple fractions.
1. Use the denominators to determine the size of the rectangle that must be built. For ¾ x ½, a rectangle with an area of 4 x 2 must be drawn.
2. Next, use the numerators to decide how much of the rectangle to look at and then shade that part. In the example, look at 3 rows by 1 column.
3. Count the shaded part to find the numerator, and then count the whole rectangle to find the denominator.
4. Write the fraction as shaded part to whole part: ³⁄₈.

Multiplying Fractions, continued

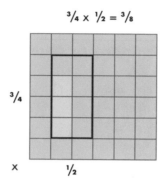

$$^3/_4 \times {}^1/_2 = {}^3/_8$$

³/₄

× ¹/₂

Parallel, Perpendicular, and Intersecting Lines

Geoboards can be used to model different lines.

★ Parallel lines are in the same plane and never meet. They are the same distance apart.

★ Intersecting lines are lines that meet or cross at a point.

★ Perpendicular lines are special kinds of intersecting lines that intersect at right angles.

  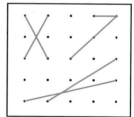

Parallel Lines   Perpendicular Lines   Intersecting Lines

Learning With Manipulatives: Geometric Solids

Building Models With Candy or Clay

This can be done with soft candies, gumdrops, or clay and some toothpicks. For larger solid models, toothpicks may need to be broken in half in order to sustain the shape.

1. Build the geometric shapes and solids: triangle, square, pentagon, hexagon, cube, triangular prism, rectangular prism, triangular pyramid, rectangular pyramid, pentagonal prism, and hexagonal prism.
2. Count the faces, edges, and vertices.
3. Extend by predicting how a film of bubble solution will cover the shape when dipped.
4. Submerge in bubble solution and check predictions.
5. If clay is used, it needs to be dense, solid clay to withstand repeated dunking.

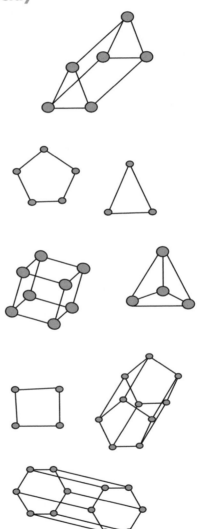

Comparing Properties

1. Make a chart or a map with one side labeled "similarities" and the other side labeled "differences."
2. Using two different geometric solids, compare and contrast the properties of the shapes.
3. Important vocabulary terms to remember when comparing and contrasting the properties include: parallel, perpendicular, faces, edges, vertices, prism, cubic, and so forth.

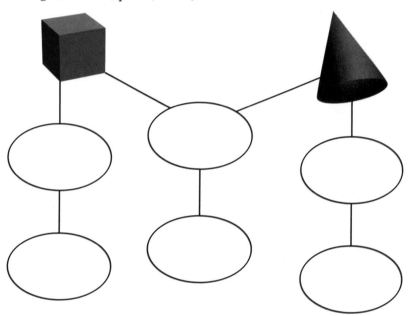

Learning With Manipulatives: Graph Paper

Dividing With Intersections

Drawing crossed lines can help find the answer to simple division problems. Graph paper helps to keep the problem neat and is easier to read and solve.

1. For 43 ÷ 6, draw 6 lines to represent 6 rows.
2. Count the number of intersections made as intersection lines are drawn to represent columns.
3. Count as close to the number as possible without going over.
4. When as many lines as possible are drawn without going over, count the number of columns drawn.
5. Count what is left over as the remainder.
6. 43 ÷ 6 has 7 columns; so the answer is 7 with a remainder of 1.

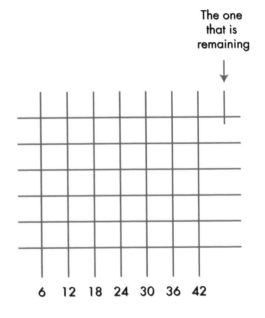

The one that is remaining

6   12   18   24   30   36   42

43 ÷ 6 = 7 columns with 1 remaining

Drawing Multiplication or Division

1. Use counters to build the problem.
2. Draw the picture out, and then write it in numbers.

Multiplying Fractions

Graph paper can be used as an intermediate step for multiplying fractions.

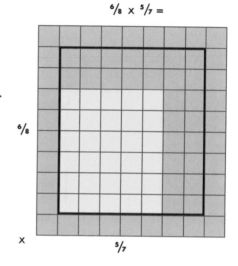

$\frac{6}{8} \times \frac{5}{7} =$

$\frac{6}{8}$

$\times \quad \frac{5}{7}$

1. Use the denominators to determine the size of the rectangle that must be drawn. For $\frac{6}{8} \times \frac{5}{7}$, a rectangle with an area of 8 x 7 must be drawn.

2. Next, use the numerators to decide how much of the rectangle to look at and then shade that part. In the example, look at 6 rows by 5 columns.

3. Count the shaded part to find the numerator, and then count the whole rectangle to find the denominator.

4. Write the fraction as shaded part to whole part: $\frac{30}{56}$.

Multiplying Intermediate 2-Digit x 1-Digit Problems

1. Draw the problem on graph paper.
2. Draw in the solution.
3. Write the answer on the grid in the drawing.
4. Write the problem and solution numerically.
5. Use a different-colored pencil to draw the problem and the solution.

Multiplying Intermediate 2-Digit x 1-Digit Problems, continued

Draw It

Write It

$$\begin{array}{r} 13 \\ \times\ 7 \\ \hline 70 \\ +\ 21 \\ \hline 91 \end{array}$$

Multiplying Intermediate 2-Digit x 2-Digit Problems

1. Draw the problem on graph paper.
2. Draw in the solution.
3. Write the answer on the grid in the drawing.
4. Write the problem and solution numerically.
5. Use a different-colored pencil to draw the problem and the solution.

Draw It

Multiplying Intermediate 2-Digit x 2-Digit Problems, continued

Write It

```
     13
   x 21
    200
     80
   +  6
    286
```

Multiplying With Window Pane Math

1. Write the problem around the outer edge of the window. Complete the simple multiplication problems and record them in the windows as shown.

2. Draw a light line through the problem when done so it isn't added by accident in the last step.

3. Finally, add the numbers within each ray, starting at the right, or the ones place, as would be done in a regular problem.

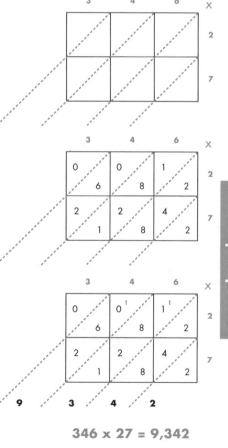

$346 \times 27 = 9,342$

Learning With Manipulatives: Hundreds Charts

Counting Multiples

Count multiples on a hundreds chart by using bingo chips or transparent game markers.

1. As each multiple of a certain number is counted orally, place a chip over the number.
2. Look for the patterns created.
3. Record the patterns on a sheet of paper.

1	2	3	4	5	6	7	8	9	10
11	12	13	14	15	16	17	18	19	20
21	22	23	24	25	26	27	28	29	30
31	32	33	34	35	36	37	38	39	40
41	42	43	44	45	46	47	48	49	50
51	52	53	54	55	56	57	58	59	60
61	62	63	64	65	66	67	68	69	70
71	72	73	74	75	76	77	78	79	80
81	82	83	84	85	86	87	88	89	90
91	92	93	94	95	96	97	98	99	100

Finding Common Multiples

1. Count multiples on a hundreds chart by using different-colored bingo chips or transparent game markers.
2. As each multiple of a certain number is counted, place a chip over the number.
3. Look for the patterns created; find the common multiples. The common multiples of two numbers are those that share two chips of different colors.
4. Record the patterns on a sheet of paper.

1	2	3	4	5	6	7	8	9	10
11	12	13	14	15	16	17	18	19	20
21	22	23	24	25	26	27	28	29	30
31	32	33	34	35	36	37	38	39	40
41	42	43	44	45	46	47	48	49	50
51	52	53	54	55	56	57	58	59	60
61	62	63	64	65	66	67	68	69	70
71	72	73	74	75	76	77	78	79	80
81	82	83	84	85	86	87	88	89	90
91	92	93	94	95	96	97	98	99	100

Learning With Manipulatives: Mirrors

Angles With Mirrors

Angles less than 180° can be measured with a hinged mirror and small object.

1. Align the mirror along an angle drawn on paper starting at the vertex.
2. Center the object in between the sides of the mirrors.
3. Count the total number of objects seen: the object on the table and those seen in the mirrors.
4. Use a calculator to divide and find the size of the angle.

Three objects total are seen, so 360 ÷ 3 = 120°.

Five objects total are seen, so 360 ÷ 5 = 72°.

Note: The drawback of this method is that it's not a precise measurement.

Line Symmetry

If a figure can be reflected, flipped, or folded over a line and it appears unchanged, that figure is said to have line symmetry. Also called reflection or fold symmetry. When folded, flipped or reflected, both sides are exactly aligned. Use a mirror to test for line symmetry.

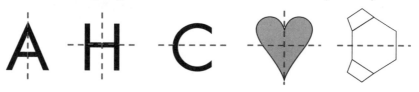

Learning With Manipulatives: Pattern Blocks

Angles

Use the standard pattern blocks to measure basic, common angles. Below is a list of the pattern block angle measurements:

★ Orange Square = 90°

★ Yellow Hexagon = 120°

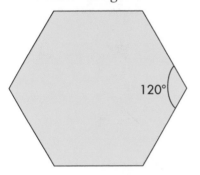

★ Small Tan Rhombus = 30°
★ Large Tan Rhombus = 150°

★ Small Blue Rhombus = 60°
★ Large Blue Rhombus = 120°

★ Small Red Trapezoid = 60°
★ Large Red Trapezoid = 120°

★ Green Triangle = 60°

Angles With Mirrors

Use hinged mirrors to determine the angles. Angle measurement is measurement from point to point on the circumference of a circle, using the center point (hinge) as the vertex.

1. Align pattern blocks along the mirror at the vertex.
2. Look into mirror at table-top level; count the block on the table and those that can be seen in the mirror. For example, using the orange square, a total of four squares can be seen.
3. Use a calculator to determine the angle: $360 \div 4 = 90°$ angle.

 Mirror hinge at vertex: When opened up, the ends of the mirror will show the shape of a circle.

 When a square is placed at the vertex, a top view will show that it's a square corner (90°) angle. Four squares total will be seen in the mirror and on the table, so $360 \div 4 = 90°$.

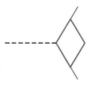 In this example, three rhombuses total will be seen, so $360 \div 3 = 120°$.

 In this example, 12 rhombuses total will be seen, so $360 \div 12 = 30°$.

Learning With Manipulatives: Pattern Blocks

Area

Area measurement is based on same-sized pieces, or units. For example, when measuring in green triangles, all shapes in a puzzle need to be converted, or measured, in green triangles. It is important to build the model and then trace it, inside and out. Avoid using the orange and tan blocks as they don't naturally cover the other shapes.

Area, continued

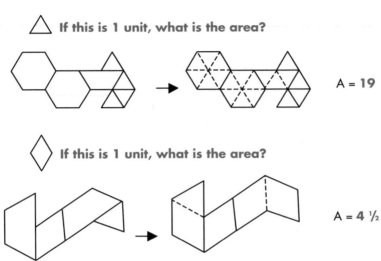

△ **If this is 1 unit, what is the area?**

A = 19

◇ **If this is 1 unit, what is the area?**

A = 4 ½

Build a shape with an area of 16 (many possible answers).

A = 16

Fractions

✪ Adding Fractions
1. Build a shape.
2. Cover it with different pieces.
3. Name those pieces by fractional size.
4. Convert those pieces to the same size.
5. Solve.

In the next example, there is more than one way to solve the problem. It can either be converted to twelfths, or it can be converted to sixths.

Fractions, continued
✪ Adding Fractions, continued

1 whole

 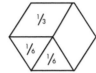

$$\tfrac{1}{6} + \tfrac{1}{6} + \tfrac{1}{3} =$$
$$\tfrac{1}{6} + \tfrac{1}{6} + \tfrac{2}{6} = \tfrac{4}{6}$$

1 whole

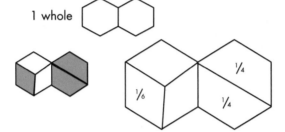

$$\tfrac{1}{6} + \tfrac{1}{4} + \tfrac{1}{4} =$$
$$\tfrac{2}{12} + \tfrac{3}{12} + \tfrac{3}{12} = \tfrac{8}{12}$$

✪ Fraction Basics 1
1. Start with the basic pattern block pieces.
2. Cover the pieces to find the fractional parts. Use a variety; for example, build ⅓, then ⅚, and then ⁴⁄₆.
3. Try to branch out. Is there another way to cover ⁴⁄₆ so that it can be named something else?

Start with one whole. Trace it.

Cover it with the largest piece possible. It can be covered with one whole hexagon, so one shape out of one shape to cover is ¹⁄₁, or 1 whole.

When covered with red, one red is ½, while both reds equal ²⁄₂, or 1 whole.

When covered with blue, one blue is ⅓, two blue are ⅔, and three blues cover the whole shape, so ³⁄₃ = 1 whole.

When covered with green, one green is ⅙, two green are ²⁄₆ or ⅓, three green are ³⁄₆ or ½, four green are ⁴⁄₆ or ⅔, five green are ⅚, and six green cover the whole thing, so ⁶⁄₆ = 1 whole.

Math Dictionary for Kids

Fractions, continued

✪ Fraction Basics 2

1. Start with the basic pattern block pieces.
2. Cover the pieces to find the fractional parts.
3. Trace and count to solve.
4. Fractions must be solved with same-sized pieces; generally, the smallest size works well.
5. Try to branch out. Is there another way to cover and name the shape?

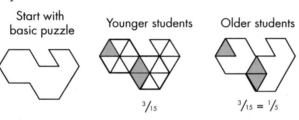

Start with basic puzzle   Younger students   Older students

$3/15$ $3/15 = 1/5$

If the trapezoid block is $1/2$, what is the following?

$1\frac{1}{2}$

If this is one unit, what is
- one green triangle? ($1/12$)
- one blue rhombus? ($2/12$, $1/6$)
- one red trapezoid? ($3/12$, or $1/4$)
- one yellow hexagon? ($6/12$, $3/6$, $2/4$, or $1/2$)

Fractions, continued

✪ Fraction Equivalence

1. Build a shape.
2. Cover it with pieces of one color.
3. Name it.
4. Cover it with pieces of another color.
5. Rename it.

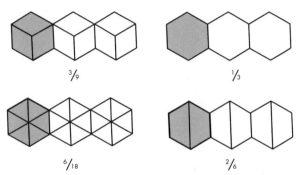

$^3/_9$ $\qquad\qquad\qquad$ $^1/_3$

$^6/_{18}$ $\qquad\qquad\qquad$ $^2/_6$

✪ Subtracting Fractions 1

★ Build a whole.
★ Cover it with the size pieces named in the problem.
★ Name those pieces by fractional size.
★ Convert those pieces to the same size.
★ Solve.

Build each part of the problem on the whole.

1 whole

$^3/_4 - ^2/_3 =$

Cover with green triangles. Count how many green triangles were left uncovered out of how many it would have taken to cover the whole. In this case, that would be 1 uncovered out of the 12 it would take to make a whole, so $^1/_{12}$.

$^3/_4 - ^2/_3 =$

$^9/_{12} - ^8/_{12} = ^1/_{12}$

Fractions, continued

✪ Subtracting Fractions 2

1. Assign each piece a value.
2. Build the problem.
3. Cover it with the size pieces named in the problem.
4. Name those pieces by fractional size.
5. Convert those pieces to the same size.
6. Solve.

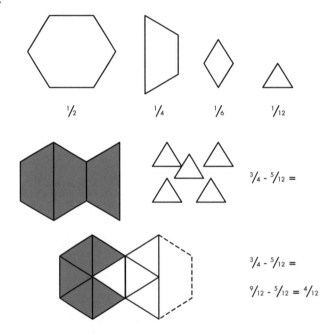

$\frac{1}{2}$ $\frac{1}{4}$ $\frac{1}{6}$ $\frac{1}{12}$

$\frac{3}{4} - \frac{5}{12} =$

$\frac{3}{4} - \frac{5}{12} =$

$\frac{9}{12} - \frac{5}{12} = \frac{4}{12}$

Build the whole and find how many green triangles it would take to cover it. That's the denominator. Then, build each part of the problem. Cover the portion being subtracted with green triangles. Count how many green triangles it would take to cover the rest. In this case, that would be 4 left out of the 12 it would take to make a whole, so $\frac{4}{12}$.

Line Symmetry

If a figure can be reflected, flipped, or folded over a line and it appears unchanged, that figure is said to have line symmetry. Also called reflection or fold symmetry. When folded, flipped or reflected, both sides are exactly aligned. Build a figure with a line of symmetry using pattern blocks, and then use a mirror to check your work.

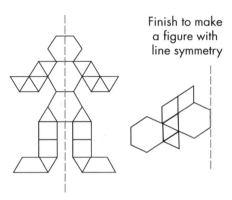

Finish to make a figure with line symmetry

Perimeter

Perimeter measurement is based on same-sized pieces, or units. In measuring perimeter with pattern blocks, the standard is the size of one side of a green triangle. The long red side equals two (2) green triangles.

The long red side has a length of two green triangles.

Find the perimeter.

P = 8

Use two blocks to build a shape with a perimeter of 9.

P = 9

Math Dictionary for Kids

Rotational Symmetry

Rotational symmetry is the number of ways a shape can be turned, or rotated, to fit on itself and still look the same. If it only fits on itself one time (a turn of 360°), it does not have rotational symmetry.

This will rotate to fit on itself two times.
That gives it a rotational symmetry of order 2.

This will rotate to fit on itself three times.
That gives it a rotational symmetry of order 3.

Learning With Manipulatives:
Protractors

Angle Measurement

A regular protractor has the shape of a half of a circle. A half a circle equals 180°, so a whole circle equals 360°. Two protractors together show a whole circle, or 360°. One is used for measuring angles less than 180°. Protractors are used to measure angles more precisely.

Learning With Manipulatives: Tangrams

Angle Identification

Tangram pieces are relational, so knowing the 90° angle can help you figure out the others. Below are the angle measurements for each piece.

★ Large triangle = 90°, 45°, 45°

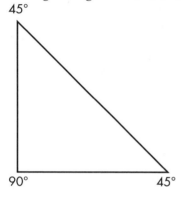

★ Small triangle = 90°, 45°, 45°

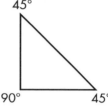

★ Square = 90°

★ Medium triangle = 90°, 45°, 45°

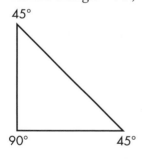

★ Parallelogram = 135°, 45°

Congruence

Congruent polygons have the same shape and the same size. The symbol for congruence is ≅.

Find two congruent triangles:

Build two congruent triangles using the following:

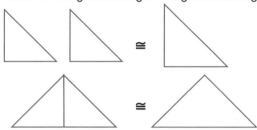

Creating Polygons

Use a specific number of tangram pieces to create given polygons. Some possibilities include:

- ★ triangles,
- ★ parallelograms,
- ★ rhomboids,
- ★ rectangles,
- ★ squares,

- ★ isosceles trapezoids,
- ★ non-isosceles trapezoids,
- ★ pentagons,

- ★ hexagons,
- ★ heptagons,
- ★ octagons,
- ★ nonagons, and
- ★ decagons.

Use five tangram pieces to make a parallelogram.

Use four tangram pieces to make an isosceles trapezoid.

Math Dictionary for Kids

Fractions

✪ Adding Fractions

1. Build shapes with tangrams.
2. Label the value of each piece. All pieces are based on the size of the small triangle, which is $\frac{1}{16}$ of the whole.
3. Add, using the basis of $\frac{1}{16}$ for conversion.

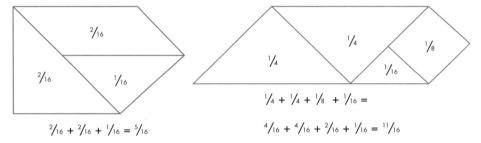

$\frac{2}{16} + \frac{2}{16} + \frac{1}{16} = \frac{5}{16}$

$\frac{1}{4} + \frac{1}{4} + \frac{1}{8} + \frac{1}{16} =$

$\frac{4}{16} + \frac{4}{16} + \frac{2}{16} + \frac{1}{16} = \frac{11}{16}$

✪ Fraction Basics 1

1. Use tangrams to find the fractional pieces of a whole. All pieces are based on the size of the small triangle, which is $\frac{1}{16}$ of the whole.
2. Determine how many small triangles it would take to make the whole square. How many large triangles would it take? How many medium triangles? How many squares?

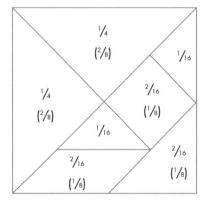

✪ Fraction Basics 2

3. Use tangrams to find the fractional pieces of a whole. All pieces are based on the size of the small triangle, which is $\frac{1}{16}$ of the whole.
4. Determine how many small triangles it would take to make various fractional parts.

Fractions, continued

✪ Fraction Basics 2, continued

If a large triangle has a value of one whole, use four pieces to find a figure with a value of 2.

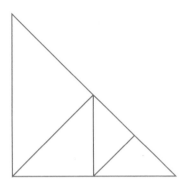

If a large triangle has a value of one whole, use three pieces to find a figure with a value of 1 ½.

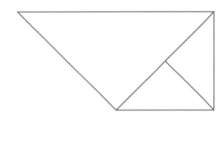

Line Symmetry

If a figure can be reflected, flipped, or folded over a line and it appears unchanged, that figure is said to have line symmetry. Also called reflection or fold symmetry. When folded, flipped or reflected, both sides are exactly aligned.

1. Build a figure with a line of symmetry using tangrams.
2. Use a mirror to check your work.

Add pieces to make a figure with line symmetry.

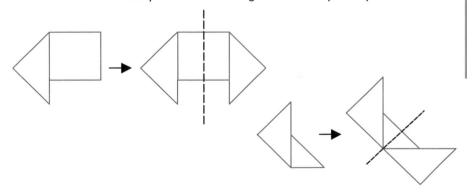

Math Dictionary for Kids

Rotational Symmetry

Rotational symmetry is the number of ways a shape can be turned, or rotated, to fit on itself and still look the same. If it only fits on itself one time (a turn of 360°), it does not have rotational symmetry.

Add more tangrams to make a polygon with rotational symmetry.

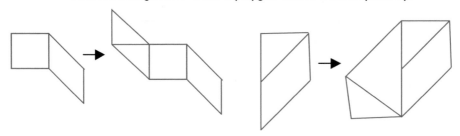

Similarity

Similar polygons have the same shape but not the same size. The symbol for similarity is ~.

Find two similar triangles:

Build two similar triangles using the following:

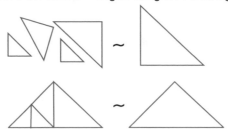

Learning With Manipulatives:
Tiles

Basic Multiplication Facts With a Class Tile Chart

This example uses the multiplication facts for the number 3.

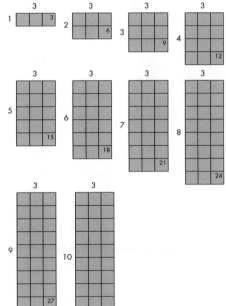

1. Use the factors 1 and 3 to build a figure with an area of 3. The figure has to be a perfect rectangle or square to be accepted.
2. Cut one out and post it on the class chart.
3. Write the factors on each side and record the total area in the bottom right corner of the shape.
4. Continue with the factors 2 and 3, then 3 and 3, and so on, until the basic facts of 3 are complete through 3 x 10.

Dividing Smaller Number Problems

1. In division, start with the total number.
2. Count out the total and put them into as many rows and columns as possible.
3. If there are leftovers, set them to the side.

Dividing Smaller Number Problems, continued

In the example shown, start by making four rows because that's the divisor. Arrange all of the tiles into those rows, until no more full rows can be made. For 22 ÷ 4, five columns can be made. When four rows of five columns are built, a total of 20 tiles are used. Subtract them from the problem. There are two tiles left, which is the remainder.

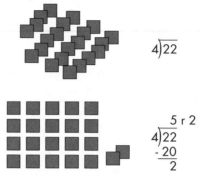

$$4\overline{)22}$$

$$\begin{array}{r} 5\ r\ 2 \\ 4\overline{)22} \\ -20 \\ \hline 2 \end{array}$$

Doubling in Multiplication

1. Build a number. The example is shown with the number 3.
2. Double one row of 3 to get two rows of 3; that makes 6.
3. Double two rows of 3 to get four rows of 3; that's 12.
4. Double four rows of 3 to get eight rows of 3; that's 24.
5. Practice doubling with all basic facts.

Formulas

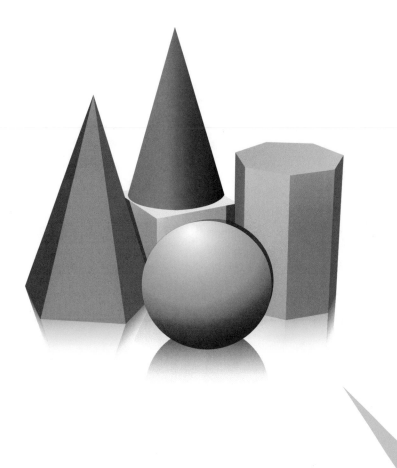

Math Dictionary for Kids

Formulas

Area

circle	$A = \pi r^2$	**r** is the radius
parallelogram	$A = b \times h$	**b** is the base, **h** is the height
rectangle	$A = l \times w$	**l** is the length, **w** is the width
square	$A = s^2$	**s** is the length of one side
trapezoid	$A = \frac{1}{2}h(b_1 + b_2)$	**b₁** and **b₂** are the opposite, parallel sides
triangle	$A = \frac{1}{2}(b \times h)$	**b** is the base, **h** is the height

Perimeter

circle	$C = 2\pi r$	**r** is the radius
	$C = \pi d$	**d** is the diameter
rectangle	$p = 2l + 2w$	**l** is the length, **w** is the width
square	$p = 4s$	**s** is the length of one side

Volume

cone	$V = \frac{1}{3}\pi r^2 h$	**r** is the radius, **h** is the height
cube	$V = s^3$	**s** is the length of one edge
cylinder	$V = \pi r^2 h$	**r** is the radius, **h** is the height
rectangular prism	$V = l \times w \times h$	**l** is the length, **w** is the width, **h** is the height
sphere	$V = \frac{4}{3}\pi r^3$	**r** is the radius

Tables and Charts

Factors of Numbers 1-10

1	1	**26**	1, 2, 13, 26	**51**	1, 3, 17, 51	**76**	1, 2, 4, 19, 38, 76
2	1, 2	**27**	1, 3, 9, 27	**52**	1, 2, 4, 13, 26, 52	**77**	1, 7, 11, 77
3	1, 3	**28**	1, 2, 4, 7, 14, 28	**53**	1, 53	**78**	1, 2, 3, 6, 13, 26, 39, 78
4	1, 2, 4	**29**	1, 29	**54**	1, 2, 3, 6, 9, 18, 27, 54	**79**	1, 79
5	1, 5	**30**	1, 2, 3, 5, 6, 10, 15, 30	**55**	1, 5, 11, 55	**80**	1, 2, 4, 5, 8, 10, 16, 20, 40, 80
6	1, 2, 3, 6	**31**	1, 31	**56**	1, 2, 4, 7, 8, 14, 28, 56	**81**	1, 3, 9, 27, 81
7	1, 7	**32**	1, 2, 4, 8, 16, 32	**57**	1, 3, 19, 57	**82**	1, 2, 41, 82
8	1, 2, 4, 8	**33**	1, 3, 11, 33	**58**	1, 2, 29, 58	**83**	1, 83
9	1, 3, 9	**34**	1, 2, 17, 34	**59**	1, 59	**84**	1, 2, 3, 4, 6, 7, 12, 14, 21, 28, 42, 84
10	1, 2, 5, 10	**35**	1, 5, 7, 35	**60**	1, 2, 3, 4, 5, 6, 10, 12, 15, 20, 30, 60	**85**	1, 5, 17, 85
11	1, 11	**36**	1, 2, 3, 4, 6, 9, 12, 18, 36	**61**	1, 61	**86**	1, 2, 43, 86
12	1, 2, 3, 4, 6, 12	**37**	1, 37	**62**	1, 2, 31, 62	**87**	1, 3, 29, 87
13	1, 13	**38**	1, 2, 19, 38	**63**	1, 3, 7, 9, 21, 63	**88**	1, 2, 4, 8, 11, 22, 44, 88
14	1, 2, 7, 14	**39**	1, 3, 13, 39	**64**	1, 2, 4, 8, 16, 32, 64	**89**	1, 89
15	1, 3, 5, 15	**40**	1, 2, 4, 5, 8, 10, 20, 40	**65**	1, 5, 13, 65	**90**	1, 2, 3, 5, 6, 9, 10, 15, 18, 30, 45, 90
16	1, 2, 4, 8, 16	**41**	1, 41	**66**	1, 2, 3, 6, 11, 22, 33, 66	**91**	1, 7, 13, 91
17	1, 17	**42**	1, 2, 3, 6, 7, 14, 21, 42	**67**	1, 67	**92**	1, 2, 4, 23, 46, 92
18	1, 2, 3, 6, 9, 18	**43**	1, 43	**68**	1, 2, 4, 17, 34, 68	**93**	1, 3, 31, 93
19	1, 19	**44**	1, 2, 4, 11, 22, 44	**69**	1, 3, 23, 69	**94**	1, 2, 47, 94
20	1, 2, 4, 5, 10, 20	**45**	1, 3, 5, 9, 15, 45	**70**	1, 2, 5, 7, 10, 14, 35, 70	**95**	1, 5, 19, 95
21	1, 3, 7, 21	**46**	1, 2, 23, 46	**71**	1, 71	**96**	1, 2, 3, 4, 6, 8, 12, 16, 24, 32, 48, 96
22	1, 2, 11, 22	**47**	1, 47	**72**	1, 2, 3, 4, 6, 8, 9, 12, 18, 24, 36, 72	**97**	1, 97
23	1, 23	**48**	1, 2, 3, 4, 6, 8, 12, 16, 24, 48	**73**	1, 73	**98**	1, 2, 7, 14, 49, 98
24	1, 2, 3, 4, 6, 8, 12, 24	**49**	1, 7, 49	**74**	1, 2, 37, 74	**99**	1, 3, 9, 11, 33, 99
25	1, 5, 25	**50**	1, 2, 5, 10, 25, 50	**75**	1, 3, 5, 15, 25, 75	**100**	1, 2, 4, 5, 10, 20, 25, 50, 100

Tables

Fraction, Decimal, and Percent Equivalents

Fraction	Decimal	Percent	Fraction	Decimal	Percent
$\frac{1}{25}$	.04	4%	$\frac{2}{5}$	.4	40%
$\frac{1}{20}$	.05	5%	$\frac{7}{16}$	.4375	43.75%
$\frac{1}{16}$	.0625	6.25%	$\frac{1}{2}$	.5	50%
$\frac{1}{15}$	$.0\overline{6}$	6⅔%	$\frac{9}{16}$	.5625	56.25%
$\frac{1}{12}$	$.08\overline{3}$	8⅓%	$\frac{3}{5}$	.6	60%
$\frac{1}{10}$	.1	10%	$\frac{5}{8}$	.625	62.5%
$\frac{1}{8}$	.125	12.5%	$\frac{2}{3}$	.66	66⅔%
$\frac{1}{7}$	$.\overline{142857}$	14%	$\frac{11}{16}$	.6875	68.75%
$\frac{1}{6}$	$.1\overline{66}$	16⅔%	$\frac{7}{10}$	.7	70%
$\frac{3}{16}$	.1875	18.75%	$\frac{3}{4}$	.75	75%
$\frac{1}{5}$	.2	20%	$\frac{4}{5}$	.8	80%
$\frac{1}{4}$	.25	25%	$\frac{13}{16}$	.8125	81.25%
$\frac{3}{10}$	.3	30%	$\frac{7}{8}$	.875	87.5%
$\frac{5}{16}$	.3125	31.25%	$\frac{9}{10}$	.9	90%
$\frac{1}{3}$	$.3\overline{33}$	33⅓%	$\frac{15}{16}$	.9375	93.75%
$\frac{3}{8}$	.375	37.5%	1	1.0	100%

Multiples of Numbers 1-50

1	1, 2, 3, 4, 5, 6, 7, 8, 9 . . .		**26**	26, 52, 78, 104, 130, 156, 182, 208, 234 . . .
2	2, 4, 6, 8, 10, 12, 14, 16, 18 . . .		**27**	27, 54, 81, 108, 135, 162, 189, 216, 243 . . .
3	3, 6, 9, 12, 15, 18, 21, 24, 27 . . .		**28**	28, 56, 84, 112, 140, 168, 196, 224, 252 . . .
4	4, 8, 12, 16, 20, 24, 28, 32, 36 . . .		**29**	29, 58, 87, 116, 145, 174, 203, 232, 261 . . .
5	5, 10, 15, 20, 25, 30, 35, 40, 45 . . .		**30**	30, 60, 90, 120, 150, 180, 210, 240, 270 . . .
6	6, 12, 18, 24, 30, 36, 42, 48, 54 . . .		**31**	31, 62, 93, 124, 155, 186, 217, 248, 279 . . .
7	7, 14, 21, 28, 35, 42, 49, 56, 63 . . .		**32**	32, 64, 96, 128, 160, 192, 224, 256, 288 . . .
8	8, 16, 24, 32, 40, 48, 56, 64, 72 . . .		**33**	33, 66, 99, 132, 165, 198, 231, 264, 297 . . .
9	9, 18, 27, 36, 45, 54, 63, 72, 81 . . .		**34**	34, 68, 102, 136, 170, 204, 238, 272, 306 . . .
10	10, 20, 30, 40, 50, 60, 70, 80, 90 . . .		**35**	35, 70, 105, 140, 175, 210, 245, 280, 315 . . .
11	11, 22, 33, 44, 55, 66, 77, 88, 99 . . .		**36**	36, 72, 108, 144, 180, 216, 252, 288, 324 . . .
12	12, 24, 36, 48, 60, 72, 84, 96, 108 . . .		**37**	37, 74, 111, 148, 185, 222, 259, 296, 333 . . .
13	13, 26, 39, 52, 65, 78, 91, 104, 117 . . .		**38**	38, 76, 114, 152, 190, 228, 266, 304, 342 . . .
14	14, 28, 42, 56, 70, 84, 98, 112, 126 . . .		**39**	39, 78, 117, 156, 195, 234, 273, 312, 351 . . .
15	15, 30, 45, 60, 75, 90, 105, 120, 135 . . .		**40**	40, 80, 120, 160, 200, 240, 280, 320, 360 . . .
16	16, 32, 48, 64, 80, 96, 112, 128, 144 . . .		**41**	41, 82, 123, 164, 205, 246, 287, 328, 369 . . .
17	17, 34, 51, 68, 85, 102, 119, 136, 153 . . .		**42**	42, 84, 126, 168, 210, 252, 294, 336, 378 . . .
18	18, 36, 54, 72, 90, 108, 126, 144, 162 . . .		**43**	43, 86, 129, 172, 215, 258, 301, 344, 387 . . .
19	19, 38, 57, 76, 95, 114, 133, 152, 171 . . .		**44**	44, 88, 132, 176, 220, 264, 308, 352, 396 . . .
20	20, 40, 60, 80, 100, 120, 140, 160, 180 . . .		**45**	45, 90, 135, 180, 225, 270, 315, 360, 405 . . .
21	21, 42, 63, 84, 105, 126, 147, 168, 189 . . .		**46**	46, 92, 138, 184, 230, 276, 322, 368, 414 . . .
22	22, 44, 66, 88, 110, 132, 154, 176, 198 . . .		**47**	47, 94, 141, 188, 235, 282, 329, 376, 423 . . .
23	23, 46, 69, 92, 115, 138, 161, 184, 207 . . .		**48**	48, 96, 144, 192, 240, 288, 336, 384, 432 . . .
24	24, 48, 72, 96, 120, 144, 168, 192, 216 . . .		**49**	49, 98, 147, 196, 245, 294, 343, 392, 441 . . .
25	25, 50, 75, 100, 125, 150, 175, 200, 225 . . .		**50**	50, 100, 150, 200, 250, 300, 350, 400, 450 . . .

Multiples of Numbers 51-100

51	51, 102, 153, 204, 255, 306, 357, 408, 459 . . .	**76**	76, 152, 228, 304, 380, 456, 532, 608, 684 . . .
52	52, 104, 156, 208, 260, 312, 364, 416, 468 . . .	**77**	77, 154, 231, 308, 385, 462, 539, 616, 693 . . .
53	53, 106, 159, 212, 265, 318, 371, 424, 477 . . .	**78**	78, 156, 234, 312, 390, 468, 546, 624, 702 . . .
54	54, 108, 162, 216, 270, 324, 378, 432, 486 . . .	**79**	79, 158, 237, 316, 395, 474, 553, 632, 711 . . .
55	55, 110, 165, 220, 275, 330, 385, 440, 495 . . .	**80**	80, 160, 240, 320, 400, 480, 560, 640, 720 . . .
56	56, 112, 168, 224, 280, 336, 392, 448, 504 . . .	**81**	81, 162, 243, 324, 405, 486, 567, 648, 729 . . .
57	57, 114, 171, 228, 285, 342, 399, 456, 513 . . .	**82**	82, 164, 246, 328, 410, 492, 574, 656, 738 . . .
58	58, 116, 174, 232, 290, 348, 406, 464, 522 . . .	**83**	83, 166, 249, 332, 415, 498, 581, 664, 747 . . .
59	59, 118, 177, 236, 295, 354, 413, 472, 531 . . .	**84**	84, 168, 252, 336, 420, 504, 588, 672, 756 . . .
60	60, 120, 180, 240, 300, 360, 420, 480, 540 . . .	**85**	85, 170, 255, 340, 425, 510, 595, 680, 765 . . .
61	61, 122, 183, 244, 305, 366, 427, 488, 549 . . .	**86**	86, 172, 258, 344, 430, 516, 602, 688, 774 . . .
62	62, 124, 186, 248, 310, 372, 434, 496, 558 . . .	**87**	87, 174, 261, 348, 435, 522, 609, 696, 783 . . .
63	63, 126, 189, 252, 315, 378, 441, 504, 567 . . .	**88**	88, 176, 264, 352, 440, 528, 616, 704, 792 . . .
64	64, 128, 192, 256, 320, 384, 448, 512, 576 . . .	**89**	89, 178, 267, 356, 445, 534, 623, 712, 801 . . .
65	65, 130, 195, 260, 325, 390, 455, 520, 585 . . .	**90**	90, 180, 270, 360, 450, 540, 630, 720, 810 . . .
66	66, 132, 198, 264, 330, 396, 462, 528, 594 . . .	**91**	91, 182, 273, 364, 455, 546, 637, 728, 819 . . .
67	67, 134, 201, 268, 335, 402, 469, 536, 603 . . .	**92**	92, 184, 276, 368, 460, 552, 644, 736, 828 . . .
68	68, 136, 204, 272, 340, 408, 476, 544, 612 . . .	**93**	93, 186, 279, 372, 465, 558, 651, 744, 837 . . .
69	69, 138, 207, 276, 345, 414, 483, 552, 621 . . .	**94**	94, 188, 282, 376, 470, 564, 658, 752, 846 . . .
70	70, 140, 210, 280, 350, 420, 490, 560, 630 . . .	**95**	95, 190, 285, 380, 475, 570, 665, 760, 855 . . .
71	71, 142, 213, 284, 355, 426, 497, 568, 639 . . .	**96**	96, 192, 288, 384, 480, 576, 672, 768, 864 . . .
72	72, 144, 216, 288, 360, 432, 504, 576, 648 . . .	**97**	97, 194, 291, 388, 485, 582, 679, 776, 873 . . .
73	73, 146, 219, 292, 365, 438, 511, 584, 657 . . .	**98**	98, 196, 294, 392, 490, 588, 686, 784, 882 . . .
74	74, 148, 222, 296, 370, 444, 518, 592, 666 . . .	**99**	99, 198, 297, 396, 495, 594, 693, 792, 891 . . .
75	75, 150, 225, 300, 375, 450, 525, 600, 675 . . .	**100**	100, 200, 300, 400, 500, 600, 700, 800, 900 . . .

Math Dictionary for Kids

Multiplication Chart

x	1	2	3	4	5	6	7	8	9	10	11	12
1	1	2	3	4	5	6	7	8	9	10	11	12
2	2	4	6	8	10	12	14	16	18	20	22	24
3	3	6	9	12	15	18	21	24	27	30	33	36
4	4	8	12	16	20	24	28	32	36	40	44	48
5	5	10	15	20	25	30	35	40	45	50	55	60
6	6	12	18	24	30	36	42	48	54	60	66	72
7	7	14	21	28	35	42	49	56	63	70	77	84
8	8	16	24	32	40	48	56	64	72	80	88	96
9	9	18	27	36	45	54	63	72	81	90	99	108
10	10	20	30	40	50	60	70	80	90	100	110	120
11	11	22	33	44	55	66	77	88	99	110	121	132
12	12	24	36	48	60	72	84	96	108	120	132	144

Prime Factors of Numbers 2-100

2	prime	**27**	3 • 3 • 3	**52**	2 • 2 • 13	**77**	7 • 11
3	prime	**28**	2 • 2 • 7	**53**	prime	**78**	2 • 3 • 13
4	2 • 2	**29**	prime	**54**	2 • 3 • 3 • 3	**79**	prime
5	prime	**30**	2 • 3 • 5	**55**	5 • 11	**80**	2 • 2 • 2 • 2 • 5
6	2 • 3	**31**	prime	**56**	2 • 2 • 2 • 7	**81**	3 • 3 • 3 • 3
7	prime	**32**	2 • 2 • 2 • 2 • 2	**57**	3 • 19	**82**	2 • 41
8	2 • 2 • 2	**33**	3 • 11	**58**	2 • 29	**83**	prime
9	3 • 3	**34**	2 • 17	**59**	prime	**84**	2 • 2 • 3 • 7
10	2 • 5	**35**	5 • 7	**60**	2 • 2 • 3 • 5	**85**	5 • 17
11	prime	**36**	2 • 2 • 3 • 3	**61**	prime	**86**	2 • 43
12	2 • 2 • 3	**37**	prime	**62**	2 • 31	**87**	3 • 29
13	prime	**38**	2 • 19	**63**	3 • 3 • 7	**88**	2 • 2 • 2 • 11
14	2 • 7	**39**	3 • 13	**64**	2 • 2 • 2 • 2 • 2 • 2	**89**	prime
15	3 • 5	**40**	2 • 2 • 2 • 5	**65**	5 • 13	**90**	2 • 3 • 3 • 5
16	2 • 2 • 2 • 2	**41**	prime	**66**	2 • 3 • 11	**91**	7 • 13
17	prime	**42**	2 • 3 • 7	**67**	prime	**92**	2 • 2 • 23
18	2 • 3 • 3	**43**	prime	**68**	2 • 2 • 17	**93**	3 • 31
19	prime	**44**	2 • 2 • 11	**69**	3 • 23	**94**	2 • 47
20	2 • 2 • 5	**45**	3 • 3 • 5	**70**	2 • 5 • 7	**95**	5 • 19
21	3 • 7	**46**	2 • 23	**71**	prime	**96**	2 • 2 • 2 • 2 • 2 • 3
22	2 • 11	**47**	prime	**72**	2 • 2 • 2 • 3 • 3	**97**	prime
23	prime	**48**	2 • 2 • 2 • 2 • 3	**73**	prime	**98**	2 • 7 • 7
24	2 • 2 • 2 • 3	**49**	7 • 7	**74**	2 • 37	**99**	3 • 3 • 11
25	5 • 5	**50**	2 • 5 • 5	**75**	3 • 5 • 5	**100**	2 • 2 • 5 • 5
26	2 • 13	**51**	3 • 17	**76**	2 • 2 • 19		

Prime Number Chart

To find prime numbers:
1. Cross off 1.
2. Circle 2, 3, 5, and 7.
3. Cross off all of the remaining multiples of 2, 3, 5, and 7.
4. Circle the numbers that are left. These are the prime numbers.

1	2	3	4	5	6	7	8	9	10
11	12	13	14	15	16	17	18	19	20
21	22	23	24	25	26	27	28	29	30
31	32	33	34	35	36	37	38	39	40
41	42	43	44	45	46	47	48	49	50
51	52	53	54	55	56	57	58	59	60
61	62	63	64	65	66	67	68	69	70
71	72	73	74	75	76	77	78	79	80
81	82	83	84	85	86	87	88	89	90
91	92	93	94	95	96	97	98	99	100

Squares and Square Roots

n	n^2		n	n^2	
1	1	1	26	676	5.099
2	4	1.414	27	729	5.196
3	9	1.732	28	784	5.292
4	16	2	29	841	5.385
5	25	2.236	30	900	5.477
6	36	2.45	31	961	5.568
7	49	2.646	32	1024	5.657
8	64	2.828	33	1089	5.745
9	81	3	34	1156	5.831
10	100	3.162	35	1225	5.916
11	121	3.317	36	1296	6
12	144	3.464	37	1369	6.083
13	169	3.606	38	1444	6.164
14	196	3.742	39	1521	6.245
15	225	3.873	40	1600	6.325
16	256	4	41	1681	6.403
17	289	4.123	42	1764	6.481
18	324	4.243	43	1849	6.557
19	361	4.359	44	1936	6.633
20	400	4.472	45	2025	6.708
21	441	4.583	46	2116	6.782
22	484	4.69	47	2209	6.856
23	529	4.796	48	2304	6.928
24	576	4.899	49	2401	7
25	625	5	50	2500	7,071

Measurement Conversion Tables

Basic Formulas

to change					to change				
inches	▸	millimeters	▸▸	x 25.4	pounds	▸	grams	▸▸	x 453.59
millimeters	▸	inches	▸▸	x 0.0394	grams	▸	pounds	▸▸	x 0.002205
inches	▸	centimeters	▸▸	x 2.54	pounds	▸	kilograms	▸▸	x 0.45359
centimeters	▸	inches	▸▸	x 0.3937	kilograms	▸	pounds	▸▸	2.205
feet	▸	meters	▸▸	x 0.3048	ounces	▸	liters	▸▸	x 0.0296
meters	▸	feet	▸▸	x 3.281	ounce	▸	cubic inches	▸▸	x 1.878
yards	▸	meters	▸▸	x 0.9144	pint	▸	liters	▸▸	x 0.4731
meters	▸	yards	▸▸	x 1.094	liters	▸	pints	▸▸	x 2.114
miles	▸	kilometers	▸▸	x 1.609	cubic inches	▸	pints	▸▸	x 0.0347
kilometers	▸	miles	▸▸	x 0.6214	pints	▸	cubic inches	▸▸	x 28.88
knots	▸	kilometers	▸▸	x 1.852	quarts	▸	liters	▸▸	x 0.9463
knots	▸	miles	▸▸	x 1.150779	gallons	▸	liters	▸▸	x 3.785
ounces	▸	grams	▸▸	x 28.349	liters	▸	gallons	▸▸	x 0.2642
grams	▸	ounces	▸▸	x 0.03527					

Celsius

| |
| freezing point of water = 0° C |
| boiling point of water = 100° C |

To convert Celsius to Fahrenheit: C x ⅘ + 32 = F

°C	°F	°C	°F	°C	°F	°C	°F	°C	°F	°C	°F
50	122	36	97	22	72	8	46	-6	21	-20	-4
49	120	35	95	21	70	7	45	-7	19	-21	-6
48	118	34	93	20	68	6	43	-8	18	-22	-8
47	117	33	91	19	66	5	41	-9	16	-23	-9
46	115	32	90	18	64	4	39	-10	14	-24	-11
45	113	31	88	17	63	3	37	-11	12	-25	-13
44	111	30	86	16	61	2	36	-12	10	-26	-15
43	109	29	84	15	59	1	34	-13	9	-27	-17
42	108	28	82	14	57	0	32	-14	7	-28	-18
41	106	27	81	13	55	-1	30	-15	5	-29	-20
40	104	26	79	12	54	-2	28	-16	3	-30	-22
39	102	25	77	11	52	-3	27	-17	1	-31	-24
38	100	24	75	10	50	-4	25	-18	-0.4	-32	-26
37	99	23	73	9	48	-5	23	-19	-2	-33	-27

Measurement
Conversion Tables

Math Dictionary for Kids

Fahrenheit

Measurement Conversion Tables

freezing point of water = 32° F boiling point of water = 212° C											
To convert Fahrenheit to Celsius: (F – 32) x ⅝ = C											
°F	°C	°F	°C	°F	°C	°F	°C	°F	°C	°F	°C
110	43	90	32	70	21	50	10	30	-1	10	-12
109	43	89	32	69	21	49	9	29	-2	9	-13
108	42	88	31	68	20	48	9	28	-2	8	-13
107	42	87	31	67	19	47	8	27	-3	7	-14
106	41	86	30	66	19	46	8	26	-3	6	-14
105	41	85	29	65	18	45	7	25	-4	5	-15
104	40	84	29	64	18	44	7	24	-4	4	-16
103	39	83	28	63	17	43	6	23	-5	3	-16
102	39	82	28	62	17	42	6	22	-6	2	-17
101	38	81	27	61	16	41	5	21	-6	1	-17
100	38	80	27	60	16	40	4	20	-7	0	-18
99	37	79	26	59	15	39	4	19	-7	-1	-18
98	37	78	26	58	14	38	3	18	-8	-2	-19
97	36	77	25	57	14	37	3	17	-8	-3	-19
96	36	76	24	56	13	36	2	16	-9	-4	-20
95	35	75	24	55	13	35	2	15	-9	-5	-21
94	34	74	23	54	12	34	1	14	-10	-6	-21
93	34	73	23	53	12	33	0.6	13	-11	-7	-22
92	33	72	22	52	11	32	0	12	-11	-8	-22
91	33	71	22	51	11	31	-0.6	11	-12	-9	-23

Math Dictionary for Kids

Kilograms

	There are 1,000 grams in a kilogram. 1 kilogram = 2.2046 pounds										

Multiply kilograms by 2.2046 = pounds						1 kilogram = the weight of about 1 liter of water					
kg	**lbs**	**kg**	**lbs**	**kg**	**lbs**	**kg**	**lbs**	**kg**	**lbs**	**kg**	**lbs**
1	2.20	21	46.30	41	90.39	61	134.48	81	178.57	101	222.67
2	4.41	22	48.50	42	92.59	62	136.69	82	180.78	102	224.87
3	6.61	23	50.71	43	94.80	63	138.89	83	182.98	103	227.08
4	8.82	24	52.91	44	97.00	64	141.10	84	185.19	104	229.28
5	11.02	25	55.12	45	99.21	65	143.30	85	187.39	105	231.49
6	13.23	26	57.32	46	101.41	66	145.50	86	189.60	106	233.69
7	15.43	27	59.52	47	103.62	67	147.71	87	191.80	107	235.89
8	17.64	28	61.73	48	105.82	68	149.91	88	194.01	108	238.10
9	19.84	29	63.93	49	108.03	69	152.12	89	196.21	109	240.30
10	22.05	30	66.14	50	110.23	70	154.32	90	198.42	110	242.51
11	24.25	31	68.34	51	112.44	71	156.53	91	200.62	111	244.71
12	26.46	32	70.55	52	114.64	72	158.73	92	202.83	112	246.92
13	28.66	33	72.75	53	116.84	73	160.94	93	205.03	113	249.12
14	30.86	34	74.96	54	119.05	74	163.14	94	207.23	114	251.33
15	33.07	35	77.16	55	121.25	75	165.35	95	209.44	115	253.53
16	35.27	36	79.37	56	123.46	76	167.55	96	211.64	116	255.74
17	37.48	37	81.57	57	125.66	77	169.76	97	213.85	117	257.94
18	39.68	38	83.78	58	127.87	78	171.96	98	216.05	118	260.15
19	41.89	39	85.98	59	130.07	79	174.16	99	218.26	119	262.35
20	44.09	40	88.18	60	132.28	80	176.37	100	220.46	120	264.55

Kilometers

There are 1,000 meters in a kilometer. 1 kilometer = 0.6214 mile = 3,280 feet											
1 kilometer = 0.6214 miles Multiply kilometers by 0.6214 = mph						1 kilometer = 0.53996 knots Multiply kilometers by 0.53996 = knots					
km/hr	mph	knots	km/hr	mph	knots	km/hr	mph	knots	km/hr	mph	knots
1	.62	0.5	14	8.7	7.6	27	16.8	14.6	40	24.9	21.6
2	1.2	1.1	15	9.3	8.1	28	17.4	15.1	41	25.5	22.1
3	1.9	1.6	16	9.9	8.6	29	18.0	15.7	42	26.1	22.7
4	2.5	2.2	17	10.6	9.2	30	18.6	16.2	43	26.7	23.2
5	3.1	2.7	18	11.2	9.7	31	19.3	16.7	44	27.3	23.8
6	3.7	3.2	19	11.8	10.3	32	19.9	17.3	45	28.0	24.3
7	4.4	3.8	20	12.4	10.8	33	20.5	17.8	46	28.6	24.8
8	5.0	4.3	21	13.0	11.3	34	21.1	18.4	47	29.2	25.4
9	5.6	4.9	22	13.7	11.9	35	21.7	18.9	48	29.8	25.9
10	6.2	5.4	23	14.3	12.4	36	22.4	19.4	49	30.4	26.5
11	6.8	5.9	24	14.9	13.0	37	23.0	20.0	50	31.1	27.0
12	7.5	6.5	25	15.5	13.5	38	23.6	20.5	51	31.7	27.5
13	8.1	7.0	26	16.2	14.0	39	24.2	21.1	52	32.3	28.1

Math Dictionary for Kids

Knots

Knots are nautical miles per hour. 1 nautical mile = 6076.12 feet = 1852 meters											
1 nautical mile/knot = 1.15077945 statute mile Multiply knots by 1.15077945 = mph						1 knot/nautical mile = 1.85200 kilometers Multiply knots by 1.85200 = kilometers					
Knots	mph	km/hr	Knots	mph	km/hr	Knots	mph	km/hr	Knots	mph	km/hr
1	1.2	1.9	14	16.1	25.9	27	31.1	50.0	40	46.0	74.1
2	2.3	3.7	15	17.3	27.8	28	32.2	51.9	41	47.2	75.9
3	3.5	5.6	16	18.4	29.6	29	33.4	53.7	42	48.3	77.8
4	4.6	7.4	17	19.6	31.5	30	34.5	55.6	43	49.5	79.6
5	5.8	9.3	18	20.7	33.3	31	35.7	57.4	44	50.6	81.5
6	6.9	11.1	19	21.9	35.2	32	36.8	59.3	45	51.8	83.3
7	8.1	13.0	20	23.0	37.0	33	38.0	61.1	46	52.9	85.2
8	9.2	14.8	21	24.2	38.9	34	39.1	63.0	47	54.1	87.0
9	10.4	16.7	22	25.3	40.7	35	40.3	64.8	48	55.2	88.9
10	11.5	18.5	23	26.5	42.6	36	41.4	66.7	49	56.4	90.7
11	12.7	20.4	24	27.6	44.4	37	42.6	68.5	50	57.5	92.6
12	13.8	22.2	25	28.8	46.3	38	43.7	70.4	51	58.7	94.5
13	15.0	24.1	26	29.9	48.2	39	44.9	72.2	52	59.8	96.3

Miles

There are 5280 feet in a mile. 1 mile = 1.6093 kilometers = 1,609.3 meters											
1 mile = 1.6093 kilometers Multiply miles by 1.6093 = kilometers						1 mile = 0.86898 knots/nautical miles Multiply miles by 0.86898 = knots					
Miles	km/hr	knots	Miles	km/hr	knots	Miles	km/hr	knots	Miles	km/hr	knots
1	1.6	0.9	14	22.5	12.2	27	43.5	23.5	40	64.4	34.8
2	3.2	1.7	15	24.1	13.0	28	45.1	24.3	41	66.0	35.6
3	4.8	2.6	16	25.7	13.9	29	46.7	25.2	42	67.6	36.5
4	6.4	3.5	17	27.4	14.8	30	48.3	26.1	43	69.2	37.4
5	8.0	4.3	18	29.0	15.6	31	49.9	26.9	44	70.8	38.2
6	9.7	5.2	19	30.6	16.5	32	51.5	27.8	45	72.4	39.1
7	11.3	6.1	20	32.2	17.4	33	53.1	28.7	46	74.0	40.0
8	12.9	7.0	21	33.8	18.2	34	54.7	29.5	47	75.6	40.8
9	14.5	7.8	22	35.4	19.1	35	56.3	30.4	48	77.2	41.7
10	16.1	8.7	23	37.0	20.0	36	57.9	31.3	49	78.9	42.6
11	17.7	9.6	24	38.6	20.9	37	59.5	32.2	50	80.5	43.4
12	19.3	10.4	25	40.2	21.7	38	61.2	33.0	51	82.1	44.3
13	20.9	11.3	26	41.8	22.6	39	62.8	33.9	52	83.7	45.2

Pounds

There are 16 ounces in a pound. 1 pound = 0.4536 kilograms											
Multiply pounds by 0.4536 = kilograms					2,000 pounds = 1 ton						
lbs	**kg**	**lbs**	**kg**	**lbs**	**kg**	**lbs**	**kg**	**lbs**	**kg**	**lbs**	**kg**
1	0.45	**21**	9.53	**41**	18.60	**61**	27.67	**81**	36.74	**101**	45.81
2	0.91	**22**	9.98	**42**	19.05	**62**	28.12	**82**	37.20	**102**	46.27
3	1.36	**23**	10.43	**43**	19.50	**63**	28.58	**83**	37.65	**103**	46.72
4	1.81	**24**	10.89	**44**	19.96	**64**	29.03	**84**	38.10	**104**	47.17
5	2.27	**25**	11.34	**45**	20.41	**65**	29.48	**85**	38.56	**105**	47.63
6	2.72	**26**	11.79	**46**	20.87	**66**	29.94	**86**	39.01	**106**	48.08
7	3.18	**27**	12.25	**47**	21.32	**67**	30.39	**87**	39.46	**107**	48.54
8	3.63	**28**	12.70	**48**	21.77	**68**	30.84	**88**	39.92	**108**	48.99
9	4.08	**29**	13.15	**49**	22.23	**69**	31.30	**89**	40.37	**109**	49.44
10	4.54	**30**	13.61	**50**	22.68	**70**	31.75	**90**	40.82	**110**	49.90
11	4.99	**31**	14.06	**51**	23.13	**71**	32.21	**91**	41.28	**111**	50.35
12	5.44	**32**	14.52	**52**	23.59	**72**	32.66	**92**	41.73	**112**	50.80
13	5.90	**33**	14.97	**53**	24.04	**73**	33.11	**93**	42.18	**113**	51.26
14	6.35	**34**	15.42	**54**	24.49	**74**	33.57	**94**	42.64	**114**	51.71
15	6.80	**35**	15.88	**55**	24.95	**75**	34.02	**95**	43.09	**115**	52.16
16	7.26	**36**	16.33	**56**	25.40	**76**	34.47	**96**	43.55	**116**	52.62
17	7.71	**37**	16.78	**57**	25.86	**77**	34.93	**97**	44.00	**117**	53.07
18	8.16	**38**	17.24	**58**	26.31	**78**	35.38	**98**	44.45	**118**	53.52
19	8.62	**39**	17.69	**59**	26.76	**79**	35.83	**99**	44.91	**119**	53.98
20	9.07	**40**	18.14	**60**	27.22	**80**	36.29	**100**	45.36	**120**	54.43

Measurement
Conversion Tables

Trivia

1 fathom = 6 feet = 1.829 meters	A knot is the measure of speed on water	1 knot is 1 nautical mile per hour	1 nautical mile = 6,080 feet = 1852 meters	1 nautical mile = 1.15 miles = 1.852 kilometers
1 gallon of gasoline weighs 6.2 pounds	1 gallon of diesel weighs 7.1 pounds	1 cubic foot of volume holds 7.48 gallons	1 cubic foot of volume will support about 60 pounds	1 cubic foot of fresh water weighs 62.5 pounds
1 statute mile = 1.609 kilometers = 1,609 meters	1 statute mile = 1,760 yards = 5,280 feet	1 kilometer = 1,000 meters	1 kilometer = 0.6142 miles = 3,290 feet	1 meter = 3.281 feet = 39.37 inches
1 yard = 0.9144 meters	1 pound = 0.45359 kilograms	1 gallon (liquid) = 3.7854 liters	1 foot = 0.3048 meters	1 inch = 2.54 centimeters

Basic Math Tools
and Equipment

Basic Math Tools
and Equipment

Although the possibilities for manipulatives are almost as limitless as the imagination, below are a few of those most commonly found in math classrooms.

AngLegs™

Anglegs™ are a set of plastic pieces in six different lengths that snap together to make various geometric shapes. These are useful for exploring polygons and angles. They can also be used to determine polygon height, area, center points, and more.

Attribute Blocks

A set of geometric shapes of various sizes and thicknesses. These can be used to learn shape recognition, patterning, spatial sense, sorting, classifying, and logical reasoning in problem solving.

Balance Scale

An instrument used for measuring weights.

Base-10 Blocks

Manipulatives based on the Base-10 number system. Three of the most commonly used pieces are very effective tools for learning counting, place value, number sense, addition, subtraction, multiplication, division, and decimals.

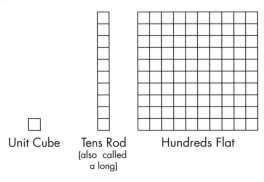

Unit Cube   Tens Rod   Hundreds Flat
(also called
a long)

Centimeter Cubes

Cubes that measure one centimeter in length, width, and height. They are useful for metric measurement and weight, as well as finding volume and surface area and in problem solving.

Compass

A tool used for drawing arcs and circles. One type has two hinged arms. One arm is pointed at the end, while the other holds a pencil. The other type of compass is called a safety compass and consists of a wider arm that rotates around a circular base.

Cuisenaire® Rods

Cuisenaire® Rods are a set of 10 different-colored rods used to learn a wide variety of concepts, including addition, subtraction, multiplication, division, fractions, area, perimeter, volume, spatial problem solving, square numbers, and equations. Based on a unit cube, these range in size from 1 unit (white) to 10 units (orange).

Dice

Dice come in a variety of colors and shapes and are numbered in a variety of ways, including the standard form, fractions, and decimals. They can be used in countless ways, such as for addition and subtraction facts, multiplication facts, fraction concepts and equivalences, probability, graphing, and a wide assortment of math games.

Basic Math Tools and Equipment

Dominoes

Dominoes come in the traditional black and white, as well as a variety of colors. They are used to build number sense, compose and decompose numbers, addition and subtraction concepts, fact families, and multiples.

Dot Paper

Paper filled with evenly spaced dots used to solve and record answers to geometry problems, especially those involving shapes, angles, and parts of circles. Dot paper is also commonly called geoboard paper.

Fraction Sets

Fraction sets come in a variety of shapes and sizes. As their name implies, fraction sets are useful tools for learning fraction concepts.

Geoboard

Geoboards are square boards with a series of pegs used to explore concepts of plane geometry, including but not limited to area, perimeter, line segments, angles, properties of plane shapes, and the characteristics of circles. Rubber bands, sometimes called geobands, are used to model the desired concepts. Some geoboards are fitted with a series of pegs in the shape of a grid on one side, while the other side has pegs in the shape of a circle. Geoboards are commonly used with dot paper.

Geoboard Paper

See *Dot Paper*.

Geometric Solids

A set of three-dimensional pieces used to explore the properties of dimensional geometric shapes. Although there are many other dimensional shapes, many sets commonly include cubes, rectangular prisms, triangular prisms, cylinders, cones, square pyramids, triangular pyramids, rectangular pyramids, tetrahedrons, and spheres. Some sets are hollow to allow for an exploration of volume, surface area, and nets.

Graph Paper

Paper separated into grids of various sizes. Graph paper can be used in basic operations to help keep problems lined up and in the exploration of multiplication and division, area, perimeter, and shapes.

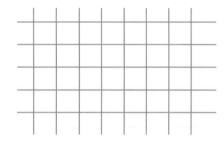

Hundreds Charts

A chart set up in a grid and numbered to teach various concepts. Some are numbered from 1 to 100, others start with zero, and still others start with a negative number. These are used to explore patterning, counting strategies, addition, subtraction, multiples, common multiples, prime numbers, and negative numbers.

1	2	3	4	5	6	7	8	9	10
11	12	13	14	15	16	17	18	19	20
21	22	23	24	25	26	27	28	29	30
31	32	33	34	35	36	37	38	39	40
41	42	43	44	45	46	47	48	49	50
51	52	53	54	55	56	57	58	59	60
61	62	63	64	65	66	67	68	69	70
71	72	73	74	75	76	77	78	79	80
81	82	83	84	85	86	87	88	89	90
91	92	93	94	95	96	97	98	99	100

Inch Cubes

Inch cubes come in a variety of colors. Measuring an inch on each side, these are useful for counting, patterning, volume, and surface area.

Mirrors

Mirrors are used to explore line symmetry and to learn the concept of angle measurement. When used in line symmetry, the mirrors are generally one piece. When used with angle measurement, they are commonly taped together to form a hinged pair.

Pattern Blocks

These are used to investigate a multitude of concepts including patterning, area, perimeter, basic fractions, equivalent fractions, adding and subtracting fractions, line symmetry, rotational symmetry, angles, properties of basic shapes, similarity, congruence, and tessellations. A set of pattern blocks comes in a container of about 250 or more and includes six basic shapes: yellow hexagon, red trapezoid, blue rhombus, green triangle, orange square, and tan rhombus.

Pentominoes

A geometric manipulative used to explore area, perimeter, symmetry, congruence, nets, and problem solving. Pentomino puzzles come in a set of 12 shapes, each made of five 1-inch squares.

Protractor

A tool used for drawing and measuring angles, most protractors are designed in the shape of a hemisphere and numbered from 0 to 180 degrees. Full circle protractors are also available, but they are not as commonly used.

Spinners

A tool that can be numbered in a variety of increments in number, color, or pattern to suit learning needs. These are often used in probability.

Tangrams

Tangrams consist of seven puzzle pieces that are put together to make a large assortment of shapes. These puzzles can be used to investigate properties of polygons, similarity, congruence, line and rotational symmetry, angles, fractions, area, perimeter, and problem solving. Each puzzle comes with two large triangles, a medium triangle, two small triangles, a square, and a parallelogram.

Tiles

Tiles are usually 1-inch square manipulatives used in counting, patterning, addition, subtraction, multiplication, division, fractional concepts, and multiplication of fractions.

Two-Color Counters

These are generally about 1 inch in diameter and have a different color on each side. Two-sided counters are used for number sense and operations, patterning, probability, addition, multiplication, division, and fractions.

Unifix Cubes®

Interlocking blocks in a 1-inch size, Unifix Cubes® come in a variety of colors. They can be used for number sense, patterning, addition, subtraction, multiplication, division, and fractions.

Math Dictionary for Kids

Index

Math Dictionary for Kids

Index

Math Dictionary for Kids

Index

Math Dictionary for Kids

Index